INVEST LIKE
A BARBARIAN

INVEST LIKE A BARBARIAN

SHARE IN THE SPOILS OF A PRIVATE MARKETS REVOLUTION

ROSS BUTLER

WILEY

This edition first published 2026
© 2026 John Wiley & Sons, Ltd

All rights reserved, including rights for text and data mining and training of artificial intelligence technologies or similar technologies. No part of this publication may be reproduced, stored in a retrieval system, or transmitted, in any form or by any means, electronic, mechanical, photocopying, recording or otherwise, except as permitted by law. Advice on how to obtain permission to reuse material from this title is available at http://www.wiley.com/go/permissions.

The right of Ross Butler to be identified as the author of this work has been asserted in accordance with law.

Registered Offices
John Wiley & Sons, Inc., 111 River Street, Hoboken, NJ 07030, USA
John Wiley & Sons Ltd, New Era House, 8 Oldlands Way, Bognor Regis, West Sussex, PO22 9NQ, UK

For details of our global editorial offices, customer services, and more information about Wiley products visit us at www.wiley.com.

The manufacturer's authorized representative according to the EU General Product Safety Regulation is Wiley-VCH GmbH, Boschstr. 12, 69469 Weinheim, Germany, e-mail: Product_Safety@wiley.com.

Wiley also publishes its books in a variety of electronic formats and by print-on-demand. Some content that appears in standard print versions of this book may not be available in other formats.

Trademarks: Wiley and the Wiley logo are trademarks or registered trademarks of John Wiley & Sons, Inc. and/or its affiliates in the United States and other countries and may not be used without written permission. All other trademarks are the property of their respective owners. John Wiley & Sons, Inc. is not associated with any product or vendor mentioned in this book.

Limit of Liability/Disclaimer of Warranty
While the publisher and the authors have used their best efforts in preparing this work, including a review of the content of the work, neither the publisher nor the authors make any representations or warranties with respect to the accuracy or completeness of the contents of this work and specifically disclaim all warranties, including without limitation any implied warranties of merchantability or fitness for a particular purpose. Certain AI systems have been used in the creation of this work. No warranty may be created or extended by sales representatives, written sales materials or promotional statements for this work. The fact that an organization, website, or product is referred to in this work as a citation and/or potential source of further information does not mean that the publisher and authors endorse the information or services the organization, website, or product may provide or recommendations it may make. This work is sold with the understanding that the publisher is not engaged in rendering professional services. The advice and strategies contained herein may not be suitable for your situation. You should consult with a specialist where appropriate. Further, readers should be aware that websites listed in this work may have changed or disappeared between when this work was written and when it is read. Neither the publisher nor authors shall be liable for any loss of profit or any other commercial damages, including but not limited to special, incidental, consequential, or other damages.

Library of Congress Cataloging-in-Publication Data is Available:

ISBN 9781394378333 (Cloth)
ISBN 9781394378340 (ePub)
ISBN 9781394378357 (ePDF)

Cover Design: Wiley
Cover Image: © Thanapon/stock.adobe.com
Author Photo: Charlotte Webb www.charlottewebbphotography.com

Set in 11.5 BemboStd by Straive, Chennai, India.
Printed and bound by CPI Group (UK) Ltd, Croydon, CR0 4YY

In Memoriam:
my cousin, Samuel Darcy Harris

Contents

Acknowledgements   ix
Foreword   xi
Preface: The Gates are Opening   xv
Mission Protocols   xxiii

PART I   Foundations   **1**

Chapter 1   A Mighty Inheritance   3
Chapter 2   The Enemy Within   21

PART II   Growth   **35**

Chapter 3   Big Beautiful Buyouts   37
Chapter 4   All Deals, Great and Small   45
Chapter 5   Real Deals and Guerrillas   55
Chapter 6   Risk It for the Biscuit   61
Chapter 7   The Rise of Free Banks   77

PART III   Access   **89**

Chapter 8   Fully Committed   93
Chapter 9   Gated Evergreens   99

Chapter 10	Listed Private Capital	109
Chapter 11	Lost in Liquidity	121
Chapter 12	Future Master of the Universe	135
Chapter 13	The Social Utility of Barbarians	143

Conclusion   *153*
About the Author   *157*
Glossary of Terms   *159*
Notes   *167*
Index   *173*

Acknowledgements

Over the course of 25 years, I have accumulated intellectual debts on the topic of private markets that are impossible to repay or fully acknowledge here. Thomas Meyer, author of the Foreword, has been influential in shaping my thinking, including through his own works, such as *Private Equity Unchained*. For a careful and critical reading of my early manuscript, I would like to thank Cyril Demaria, Sam Barton, James Burnham, Faith Tibble and Don Chew. Their unflinching feedback greatly improved the final product. Thanks to Roger Blears for his thoughts and guidance on tax-advantaged vehicles and thanks to Hans Lovrek for first making me aware of the parallels between the ancient commenda and modern private equity. I owe much to my early mentors and editors, Shaun Beaney and Grant Murgatroyd, who first introduced me to venture capital and private equity, and also to my former colleagues of the EVCA and the many industry volunteers I had the pleasure of working with in Brussels during the GFC. And in one fell swoop, I would like to thank all the many private markets professionals who have shared their knowledge with me on the 'Fund Shack' podcast – this book would have been much harder to write without these first-hand insights. May I also thank my publisher, Wiley, for enabling me to address a gap in private markets literature that speaks to the citizen investor. Above all, I thank my wife. Without her boundless support, encouragement and patience, I may have stayed on shore, forever wondering what was beyond the horizon.

Ross Butler, September 2025

Foreword

Barbarians at the Gate, the 1989 book on KKR's leveraged buyout of RJR Nabisco by investigative journalists Bryan Burrough and John Helyar, sets the theme for Ross Butler's book. Barbarians have a bad reputation, but, in fact, they share the ability to adapt and thrive under extreme uncertainty and amid unforeseeable circumstances – as is the case with the private capital industry.

This is not the typical 'how to get rich quick' by playing the private markets: if you want to be successful, you must first thoroughly understand the rules of the game, particularly if you invest as an individual. Ross Butler brings years of professional experience, and his book goes a long way in clarifying these rules – warts and all.

A Large Investment Universe, in Theory

Ross begins by reflecting on the historical roots of private markets – an approach that is both entertaining and provides a solid foundation for understanding the timeless nature of these rules. It is estimated that in 2024, there were nearly 25 times more privately backed companies than those listed in public markets. However, the total capitalisation of organised private equity is just some 12% of public equity markets.

One could argue that individuals benefit from private market returns indirectly through their pension and life insurance schemes. However, individuals increasingly seek more direct exposure to unique, high-growth companies that are not available through stock markets. This is not only for financial returns but also to support early-stage and innovative businesses, which all members of society have some stake in. Family and friends (and fools) attempt this as 'business angels', generally with marginal success, since it requires skills and time – that most individuals don't have. Meanwhile, taking part in options and share programmes of employers can be an opportunity to share success with an entrepreneurial start-up, but it leads to a high concentration of one's fortunes. Overall, most individual investors are insufficiently served by these avenues into private markets.

But Difficult to Access for Small Investors

Since the mid-2000s, investment into private markets funds has seen hyper-growth. This has precipitated an almost Darwinian struggle with an accelerating (and often confusing) 'speciation' into various forms of investment vehicles. From an institutional perspective, limited partnership funds – the 'classical' closed-end funds with capital calls and a fixed lifespan – dominate, with $5.8 trillion in assets under management at the end of 2024.[1]

Individuals can access the marketplace through publicly listed private capital managed by various buyout and venture capital firms. However, the assets under their management in these listed vehicles are a smaller proportion of this – just $600 billion.[2] Unlisted evergreen funds – open-ended funds with unrestricted lifespans – also cater for the needs of smaller investors, but at the time of writing, account for just $200 billion – a fraction of the private investment universe.

Too Risky?

What makes these avenues in private markets attractive for smaller investors is that private market risks tend to be exaggerated. Researchers and observers suggest that even during periods of market disruptions and heightened volatility, such as the dotcom crash and the Great Financial Crisis, in relative terms, private equity outperformed global public markets by a noticeable margin. Particularly, a major component of risk – correlations between public and private markets – is rarely discussed and is poorly understood.

Private funds offer investors insulation from volatility and sentiment in public markets. This is because capital is 'committed' to such funds and even if its investors lose confidence in the portfolio's current state, the fund managers are not forced to sell into public markets when valuations are down. Per se, market volatility therefore has no detrimental impact on private fund performance. An investor that is under no obligation to sell and decides to remain committed to a diversified portfolio of private funds until they mature is exposed to little capital risk (i.e. the chances of not getting their invested capital – plus a premium – back). Taking this long-term perspective means keeping short-term liquidity risks under control.

Barbarians versus Nobility

Nevertheless, like all good things, the private capital industry too must be approached with prudence. Decades of booming investments have turned private markets into their own fiefdom. Previously, the private equity industry had a private-to-public (and vice versa) conversion function, notably in the form of stock market listings. This function has been dwindling in recent years; increasingly, acquisitions and new ventures are private-to-private.

The industry may be returning to the ancient roots Ross describes, which one industry expert has even referred to as a 'noble business'. Already in 2006, an article in *The Economist* found KKR's Henry Kravis to be a 'Barbarian no more' and that, increasingly, 'private' is turning into 'privileged' equity. The industry aims to operate without the burden of public transparency and with a preference for secrecy; its growth is coinciding with a strengthening libertarian movement, particularly among Silicon Valley CEOs, opposed to any form of constraint and government interference. The business model of private equity is heavily built on the advantages of 'connections', which in the extreme can turn into cronyism.

The Democratisation of Private Equity

In private markets, many of the 'rules' are not drawn up by governments and regulators but by those who have 'skin in the game' – and hold the cards. These rules – and their enforcement – depend on trust, fairness and alignment of interests. Without understanding this and how to navigate this landscape, smaller investors tend to be at a disadvantage.

Ross's description of a dystopian investment world, where large institutional investors and sovereign wealth funds of foreign, sometimes totalitarian, states extract the economic benefits from our economy, is closer to the current state of affairs than many realise.

The opening up of private markets to more investors and market players is an antidote to this trend towards exclusion and extraction.

The 'democratisation' of private markets gives hope, as it constitutes a seismic shift in the investment landscape, expanding the investable universe for ordinary citizens and opening up access to the real economy. Individuals can now use it to invest in aspirational, lightly regulated, and value-creating private enterprises and can take a stake in the future success of their economies.

Over the last two decades, Ross and I have been fellow travellers in the private market's 'barbarian' world, and his book tells the story that covers many of our discussions over the years. Like a modern-day Marco Polo, Ross describes an epic landscape and maps out the routes for us to follow. Safe travels!

Thomas Meyer, July 2025

Preface: The Gates are Opening

If you aren't familiar with private markets, then you aren't seeing the full picture.

The fact is that any investment portfolio that focuses only on stocks and bonds is operating in an ever-more concentrated theatre of investment.

There is a vast universe of opportunity outside of these 'public markets' that has been largely hidden from most individual investors. This is the world of *private* markets fund management, which, for decades, has given privileged access to unlisted investments for an international institutional elite.

Now that is changing.

The gates to the big wide world of investment are creaking open – not to let you in, but to let you out. Private markets fund managers can give you access to the boundless productivity and growth of private enterprise – not just those well-known companies within the confines of the stock exchange or those public offerings from corporations that are large enough to raise bonds on the global capital markets.

These fund managers are not constrained by public 'listings' or size – they can invest into start-ups and alongside entrepreneurs in private companies, long before they become large enough to 'float' on the stock market; they can buy family-owned companies; they can provide loans to businesses (once the preserve of regulated banks); they can acquire real estate, infrastructure assets and utilities. Their opportunity-set is literally unconstrained. And now, through them, you can access these opportunities too.

The big institutions that have been enjoying private markets assets these past few decades have been rapidly increasing their exposure to it, to the extent that a 20% portfolio allocation to private markets is now considered a norm – while some institutions allocate 40% or more.[1] If they do, why shouldn't you? Well, it's not for everybody, but it *is* for anybody. The question I want to help you answer is whether it's for *you*.

Nobody Is on Your Side

Yes, the opportunity is vast, but I will not make any predictions about what your returns will be. Private markets funds managers tend to make bold claims about performance, while their many detractors in the financial and media establishments typically overstate the downsides. For instance, there is a long-running debate about whether private markets outperform public markets – I would advise you to ignore it.

You don't have to believe the hype to allocate to private markets. All you need to do is look around – see what is happening to stock markets across the world (concentrated, stifled by regulation, losing market share) and where the most productive companies are turning for capital (yes, to private markets).

That does not mean you will *definitely* achieve better returns investing in private than public markets. All investments are uncertain. It does mean that if you want investment exposure that is broadly reflective of the productive potential of the economy, you can no longer do so with an exclusively public markets focus.

But I will make one 'outrageous' claim on behalf of private markets: I believe they create vastly more socio-economic value, dollar-for-dollar, than the mainstream public and capital markets. How much of this outperformance will be passed on to you, the end-investor (after fees, for instance), is not something that can be satisfactorily resolved in the abstract or by looking at averages.

To the return-focused investor, I will simply say that while it may feel like a neutral position to sit on the sidelines or to wait-and-see, avoiding private markets increasingly means taking on a riskier, more concentrated position.

Are Individuals More Foolish than Institutions?

There is a widely held (and patronising) assumption that individual investors are less capable of making good decisions than institutional investors.

Typically, the distinction is drawn through the use of the word 'sophisticated'. But sophistication is a poor proxy for the ability to make good decisions. It is to emphasise cleverness over wisdom.

One justification for the assumption that institutions are better at taking risks than individuals is that they have internal checks and balances. But they are also bureaucracies that invest according to policies, which are applied by committees, which are run by people who have their own agendas and these will always be different in some way from that of the ultimate beneficiary.

The irony is that much private markets activity is predicated on the fact that bureaucratic ways of doing business lead to exploitable inefficiencies. Often, I have spoken to private equity executives about a deal, and they can barely contain their glee that they found such an easy way to make big returns that nobody else saw – and so often it was because they correctly identified policy-driven bureaucratic behaviour that made no economic sense – and fixed it.

This idea of sophistication or a lack of it goes hand in hand with the modern justification for much financial regulation: that investors need protecting. One problem with this is that, beyond overseeing basic good conduct, regulators are very bad at judging investment risk. For instance, by 'protecting' investors from making long-term commitments in private markets, regulators in many countries have been inadvertently encouraging them to make short-term bets and turning a market for investment into a casino of capital.

In some countries, where cultures and regulatory environments have been less biased against long-term investment (France and Italy, for instance), individual investors have been more active in private markets for many decades. But even there, it has always been something of a minority sport – typically the preserve of the very wealthy or people 'in the know'.

The good news is that today, the market is opening up to everyone, in a trend that is termed the 'democratisation' of private markets. You don't need to have millions (although it doesn't hurt).

Why 'Barbarians'?

Barbarians. The word comes from how Greeks thought non-Greek speakers sounded. 'Ba-bas'. The Romans – and later the Chinese and the English – later took it on to mean any uncivilised people beyond the borders of empire. A few millennia later, it's how any established institution denigrates newcomers and threats to its power.

In the financial world, it is a term that has attached itself to private equity, following the 1989 best seller, *'Barbarians at the Gates'*, describing the de-listing and buyout of a publicly listed tobacco company, RJR Nabisco. In that tale, a private equity firm called KKR was the 'barbarian'; the wasteful managers of the tobacco company were the Romans. The title was meant to be at least somewhat ironic. But in the decades since, the irony has been lost and the moniker has stuck.

Private equity firms are sometimes characterised as rapacious corporate raiders – breaking up companies and enriching themselves, with little regard for employees, company pensions or corporate continuity. Their cousins and forebears in venture capital, which backs start-ups and entrepreneurs with seed money so they can become the tech giants of tomorrow, are viewed with more ambivalence, but even they do not entirely escape the mistrust of the corporate establishment. More recently, private credit firms are referred to by the establishment as 'non-banks' and 'shadow banks'. Private markets fund managers are the ultimate disruptors, anti-establishment creative-destructors. I will argue that their bad reputation is the surest sign of the good they do and the socio-economic value they can create.

What Makes Private Markets Successful?

Empires are very stable until they aren't. And because imperial institutions are built for stability, not instability, when they fall, they fall hard. The life of the barbarian is different. They confront uncertainty all the time, and a successful barbarian is one that develops institutions that are adaptive, anti-fragile and are able to thrive amid unforeseeable circumstances. Modern scholarship has discovered that Genghis Khan was so astonishingly successful (his empire was five times larger than Alexander the Great's, and he conquered more people in a couple of decades than the Roman Empire managed in four centuries) precisely because he developed systematic behaviours for each of his conquests.[2] For instance, he would identify talented individuals, scholars and true technical experts from among conquered nations and would raise their social standing within the growing Mongol empire. At the same time, he ruthlessly dispensed with the decadent and ineffectual aristocracy.

Managing an empire is a bureaucratic exercise, but building an empire from the dust, that is a people business. Good private investment is not a financial exercise and it's not an exercise in compliance; it's about the right management of incentives and the alignment of interests. That's why anyone can understand the fundamentals of private markets without any special knowledge.

But although private market investment is a people business, the success of private markets is not a story about a few individuals. There is no Warren Buffett of private equity, no superstar innovator, no Elon Musk or Steve Jobs, there is just a diverse bunch of people who discovered a well-adapted, naturally evolved strategy and who have, as a consequence, now become the new Kings of Capitalism, the Masters of the Universe or, less hyperbolically, just ordinary everyday parts of the capital markets ecosystem.

They have this power because they are the beneficiaries of an inheritance of inestimable value: an investment structure that is the best kept secret in the investment world; a structure that is rarely discussed, and when it is, it is often misrepresented, and yet it is the single most important feature of private markets, used by all, from the smallest venture capitalists up to the largest buyout groups. It does not offer a formula for investment success, but it does offer an arrangement for delegating responsibilities and aligning incentives that has proven an astonishingly effective way of containing risks and driving returns. Whatever claims you may have heard about the performance of the private equity industry, whatever names you might associate it with, the fundamental bedrock of value in the industry comes down to that uncoolest of things: its fund structure.

The hero of this book is not a person but a set of processes that have emerged very slowly over the course of centuries, through trial and error, to exploit opportunity while managing risk. Most recently, it has been subsumed by a band of Wall Street outsiders, private markets investors and barbarians who perpetually disrupt the established order in an exemplar of 'creative destruction'.

Private markets funds are very unorthodox. They are designed to operate for a decade or so and then self-terminate. Investors get their money back (plus whatever profits have been made), but only when the fund manager is good and ready to give it – not 'on demand'. Those are the rules of barbarian life.

If private equity investors are barbarians, then the classical 10-year closed-end fund is their sword, their shield, their supply train, their system for incentivising and rewarding their warriors, the mechanism for ensuring discipline, for containing overreach, for protecting and nurturing conquered territories and for paying tribute where it is rightfully due. But since they are not barbarians but white-collar workers with high standards in personal hygiene, this private markets system of governance and alignment is something altogether more powerful. It is a foundation of demonstrable economic value creation in a free market.

Why Are the Gates Opening?

Restrictive regulations in much of the Anglosphere, as well as technical difficulties regarding fund structuring, have made it difficult for individuals to invest in private markets.

But in recent years, two things have happened.

Firstly, regulators in the United States and the United Kingdom have largely reversed their historic prejudice against long-term investments, and in some cases are now encouraging such access – even for retail investors.

And secondly, fund managers have created ways to provide simple and cheap access to private markets for anyone. The big institutions that have historically provided capital to funds have begun to max out their allocation to private markets, so fund managers are desperately seeking new sources of capital. That's why they are now making special efforts to attract capital from individual investors like you.

Meanwhile, there are several pull-factors: most importantly, there are investment opportunities that are crying out for private fund capital. For instance, there is a huge demand for credit, now that lending has become much more expensive for traditional banks in the wake of regulation in response to the Global Financial Crisis. As a result, private credit funds have emerged from almost nowhere to become a major force in the lending markets, taking on big banks with their rising costs of capital and expensive infrastructure, and winning market-share in everything from small business lending right through to blue-chip investment grade loans and even consumer finance.

Another driver is the massive demand-pull of infrastructure investment, as cash-strapped and heavily indebted governments look to patient private market players to fund long-term projects.

In addition, as private markets continue to steal market-share from the corporate models that dominated the 20th century, individual investors now have the chance to be beneficiaries of the next wave of private markets investment. For instance, private equity ownership has become a preferred alternative to stock market listings for ambitious business executives – that's why many of the best entrepreneurs and business executives want to be backed by private equity funds.

Taken as a whole, this 'democratisation' of private markets constitutes a seismic shift in the investment landscape. It's not every day that a whole new area of the economy comes online for individuals to invest in. It effectively expands the investable universe for ordinary citizens from a finite pool of publicly traded assets and opens up access to the aspirational, lightly regulated, value-creating real economy of private enterprise. You can now begin to take a stake in the future success of their economies and to be where the action happens.

While this opportunity to invest in private markets may *seem* highly novel and therefore, perhaps, risky, it is worth considering that it is the public markets that would be unrecognisable to investors of the past, with its high-frequency trading, pump-and-dump, short positions, bloated and bland reporting, central-bank-driven pricing, myriad rules, regulations and investor 'protections'. That's why the subtitle of this book is literal. We are seeing a private markets *revolution* – I'll show you that true private investment is coming around again, although this time, with greater sophistication and ever more battle-tested structures.

How This Book Is Structured

This book is in three parts. The first part, 'Foundations', will explain the fundamental nature of private markets, some historical parallels and use cases, and will deal with the main conceptual differences between this and the world of highly tradeable (aka 'public') assets, like the stock markets.

The second part, 'Growth', looks at how private markets create value.

And the third part, 'Access', looks at the different ways you can invest in private markets – whether you are super-rich or just want to set aside some capital for the future. Broadly, the choices are to invest directly into classical closed-ended 'limited partnership' funds, into unlisted evergreen funds, or into a stock market listed proxy. All these approaches give you real exposure to the productive economy and they all, as you might expect, have their pros and cons. And if you want to go a step further and not just invest like a barbarian, but *become* one – through career in private markets or by setting up your own private capital firm, we look at that too.

Why You Should Read It

Empires create fortunes for a tiny number of people, and they also create slaves. That's because they are centralised and extractive. The modern financial system is highly centralised. The market for equity is concentrated in a tiny number of big companies, and most of it is held and controlled by a few asset managers, index providers and proxy voting companies. Meanwhile, the market for credit has been even more centralised: regulated and licensed banks have had a chokehold on lending to the productive economy for many decades.

Private markets smash through that. They channel money into the hands of business founders, entrepreneurial managers and exciting investment projects. It has been called a billionaire factory for those managing funds, but it is something much more important than that. It's a *millionaire* factory for the entrepreneurs it backs, the top talent they attract, the consultants that advise them and, with sufficient patience, the investors that commit to them.

Private markets are the single greatest decentralising phenomenon of our age. It is a vehicle for upward social mobility and broad wealth creation. If you want to be part of that particular warband and share in the spoils of an adventure that promises to rescue a forlorn financial system from itself while delivering capital into the hands of the truly deserving and most productive ideas and entrepreneurs, this is the book for you.

Mission Protocols

Field Manual

Entering barbarian territory
Before heading into barbarian-controlled territory, take some time to learn the language and customs you will encounter. It may seem somewhat foreign at first, it will soon become second nature.

Combatants & materiel

Fixed-life funds

These are the classic fund types used by private markets managers. They are 'one-voyage' vehicles of about ten years, during which time it will make a dozen or more investments, return capital and profits back to investors, and is then de-commissioned. Mainly referred to as 'LP' funds. They require a big commitment from each investor. Pretty much everything that's complex and valuable about private markets comes down to this cumbersome vessel.

LP (Limited Partner)

An investor in an 'LP' fund – the vehicle of choice for the modern barbarian. LP investors are usually institutions or the ultra-wealthy. They fund the round-trip but 'stay at home'.

GP (General Partner) – The fund manager

The private markets fund manager / ship's captain / barbarian. They raise capital and venture into unlisted waters to find deals and (hopefully) create value and profits.

Liquidity

The tradability of an investment. Underlying assets in private markets are highly 'illiquid' – i.e. they cannot be traded easily. This is the reason that private markets investment requires commitment and patience on the part of investors.

Evergreen funds

Unlike fixed-life funds, these vehicles don't have to 'return home' to the investor with proceeds every time they realise a profit, they can just keep re-investing proceeds.

Underlying assets

The investments made and assets acquired by the fund. In private *equity*, often referred to as 'portfolio companies'.

'Semi-liquid' funds

A type of open-ended evergreen fund giving direct exposure to underlying assets. But the name is a misnomer: these are illiquid and only contingently redeemable and non-tradeable. I refer to them as 'gated evergreens'.

Listed private capital companies

Stock-market listed companies that provide exposure to private markets through a public equity stock. It's a proxy, but it is ultra-low hassle and requires the smallest commitment of all ($100 would do it) – and it's 'liquid'. There are two main types: listed managers and listed funds.

Carried interest

The GP's share of the booty. Usually 20%. But if they don't make at least 8% returns a year on the investments overall, it doesn't pay out. Also called 'carry'.

2/20

If they don't achieve their 20% carry, they'll still get the '2': that's 2% of the fund per year for their labour.

Strategies – Find Your Tribe

Venture capital
Financing high-potential, pre-revenue or loss-making start-ups for an equity stake.

Growth capital
Financing high-growth, post-revenue, sometimes profitable companies for an equity stake.

Private equity
Acquiring profitable, cash-generative companies for a majority ownership stake.

LBOs
Not really a type of investment, just a technique used by private equity funds to acquire companies by raising debt backed by the target company's own assets, to fund the purchase.

Private credit
Debt capital provided by private funds. This really makes them 'private banks', but that name's taken so I use 'free banks'.

Private real assets
Financing for profitable, cash-generative assets such as real estate, infrastructure, utilities, as well as natural resources, forestry, etc.

Secondaries
Acquisitions of second-hand interests in classical closed-end funds (often at a discount to their face value).

Co-investment
Investing alongside a 'GP', usually without paying fees, but still passively.

Continuation funds
A single-asset fund with one purpose: to allow a GP to continue to own an asset after the original closed-end fund has expired.

GP stakes
Buying equity stakes in the GP's fund management company. Niche, but popular. It's a bit like investing in a stock exchange itself, rather than companies listed on it.

Know Thyself

Retail
Anybody with a few shekels to invest.

Mass affluent
Those with several $100k to invest.

High-net-worth individuals
Mini-millionaires

Ultra-high-net-worths
Modern Medicis

Accredited/qualified/sophisticated investors
Bureaucratic definitions that differ by jurisdiction. Typically for the higher end of mass affluent and upwards, but you must also demonstrate some sentience. I will use the term 'accredited'.

Family office
A private investment vehicle that pools and invests money for a very rich person, family or group of families.

Now that you are armed with the essentials and protocols, acquaint yourself with the mission.

Mission Briefing

Operation: Invest like a barbarian
Classification: Private

1. **Situation**
   a. **Enemy forces:** Inflation, opportunity cost, concentration, investment risk, fees, liquidity mismatch, misinformation.
   b. **Friendly forces:** Productive private enterprises, competitive credit markets, aligned incentives, governance.
   c. **Weather & terrain:** Changeable, perma-crisis. Deploy all-weather strategies.
   d. **Civil and governance:** Socio-economic impact of activities to be aligned with returns. Manager compensation to be aligned with investor outcomes.
2. **Mission**
   To ascertain whether private markets are 'worth it' – and what proportion of capital to allocate; to select an investment vehicle type (e.g. listed PE, unlisted evergreen, closed-end fund).
3. **Execution**
   a. Explore private markets provenance and governance (Chapters 1–2)
   b. Analyse return dynamics from different strategies (Chapters 3–7)
   c. Identify potential entry points (Chapters 8–12)
   d. Assess impact on local population (Chapter 13)
   e. Sit-rep (Conclusion)

May honour and glory attend you.

Part I

Foundations

*I*n an ideal world, you wouldn't invest through private markets funds, you'd just go straight to the source and invest in companies yourself, by doing deals with entrepreneurs for an equity stake, or providing them with a loan. This would make you a 'business angel' (or, I suppose, a 'loan shark'). It would cut out the middlemen, avoid the fees and would require no regulation or compliance. It might also be enjoyable. It is also an incredibly risky and laborious activity – generally popular among high-net-worth individuals with time and money to lose[1].

The advantage of private markets is that these tasks are performed by a professional fund manager who selects and manages pools of such assets in a way that optimises the return and minimises operational risk.

Private markets funds are a conduit for you to invest capital in the most promising opportunities across the productive economy, in a way that leverages engaged ownership, good corporate governance and supportive lending practices. This also means it's very good for the economy because it channels capital to the most deserving – which is, surely, a core purpose of the investment industry.

This way of investing in private companies might sound novel, but it's not actually new, in essence. It is more like a return to the old way of investing in companies and of lending to them – not through standardised products that can be instantly traded via numbers on a screen, but through real, human engagement.

In the first chapter, we are going to trace the provenance of private markets over the course of civilisation. You don't need to know a thousand years of history *in order to invest in private markets, but I think it helps. (I am wary of innovation in financial markets.)*

Then we will look at the symbiotic nature of public and private markets and their current malfunction. And finally, we will look at LBOs: the way private equity firms acquire large corporations.

1

A Mighty Inheritance

Miranda: 'O brave new world, that has such people in it'
Prospero: 'Tis new to thee'.
— **The Tempest, William Shakespeare**

Private markets are a way of investing in a private company that is held by a fund manager in a *partnership* with investors. This brings together the benefits of private company ownership with those of professional fund management – and all without the distractions, regulations, bureaucracy and diverging interests of atomised public ownership. It is time-tested and adapted for the uncertainties involved in making investments in the productive parts of the economy.

Given the rapid growth of private markets, there are seemingly new innovations and structures on a daily basis – but the fundamental governance structures remain remarkably consistent and draw on an ancient provenance.

Private equity is probably the best-known strategy in the private markets sphere, but all strategies share a similar fundamental fund structure.

In a nutshell, a private equity firm raises funds from a bunch of big institutions, and over the course of a few years, uses them to buy a dozen or so companies. It spends several years working with the management teams of those companies to make them bigger, better, more profitable, and then sells them, locking in a capital gain and returns all the capital to investors. If the total return from the fund, after all the companies are sold, is good and the investors are pleased, the private equity firm gets to raise another fund. Rinse and repeat.

Under this investment model, the private equity manager is given a lot of freedom and has a lot of control – in terms of time, resources and initiative – to execute their investment strategy. The freedom comes from the fact that the capital is committed but not 'invested', so they can take their time and choose from a large pool of companies. The fund also centralises work and allows costs to be shared among all investors – for finding companies and conducting due diligence, for instance.

When they do decide to invest in a company, they don't take microscopic stakes, as public market investors do. They buy a majority share in each company. So the private equity firm is in control and can ensure each business is managed in the interests of its owners.

This is a major advantage. If you – or the fund you have invested in – acquires less than 1% of a company, it's a bit of a stretch to call yourself an owner or even a part owner. (In fact, many legal scholars argue that stock market investors are not, in fact, owners, at all.) In such situations, even a large institutional investor will have very little (if any) say in how the company is run. But if you own 50% or more of a company, as private equity investors do, there is a very clear connection between ownership and control. This means the company can be run in the interests of its beneficial owners (including you), not for the benefit of the salaried agents employed to run it.

The entrepreneurs and top executives in the underlying companies are given five or so years to make the company much more valuable. If they do, they get very rich. If they don't, they get fired and replaced sharpish. Then it is sold to a third party, at which point, all the spoils are returned to the investors and the fund is wound up.

This requirement means there is no ambiguity about the value that has been created, since cash flows back to the fund and, for classical closed-end funds, all the way back to the end-investor.

There are four main reasons that this model has been so successful.

The first is that the capital is not initially put to work, it is just committed. This fact gives the private equity firm a huge amount of latitude to invest where they see value. And because they are investing in private companies, the available opportunity-set is vast. Rather than picking between a finite pool of heavily trawled listed companies all swimming in the same shallow pond, private equity firms can fish from the cool dark waters of a vast ocean of opportunity.

The second is that the fund doesn't go on forever, like most funds. Once the companies are sold, the money can't be reinvested in something else – it has to be returned to investors, who get their money back. In the final analysis, there need be no valuation guess work involved. It's just *did you return the money or not?* The private equity guys have to make themselves redundant and then start all over again. It's massively inefficient and incredibly powerful because it keeps everyone honest and on their toes.

The third reason is that the main compensation arrangement for both the private equity managers and the underlying company managers is a share of the profits from the realisation of each company. And they have to invest some of their own money (their 'co-investment') into the fund for this to happen (and for company managers or younger barbarians, this may involve a remortgage or a big loan). This alignment of interest with the ultimate investors is both controversial and absolutely essential to private equity performance. It is often called having 'skin in the game'.

The fourth reason is that the private equity firms have control. There is much less of an agency problem, as there is in public markets, where the executives of listed companies can enrich themselves and engage in vanity projects at the expense of shareholders (a problem that has been identified in theory and practice for more than a century). By contrast, if private equity backed managers don't perform for their beneficial owners and liege lords, they're out.

A Curious Partnership

Classical private markets funds are structured as partnership agreements. These are closed-end, one-voyage vehicles. They venture out on the high seas of enterprise, make investments and return to shore where they unload all profits.

Most individuals will invest in feeders to these funds, which will have many advantages, which we will come on to. But for now, we will look at these one-voyage vehicles because they are the tip of the spear.

In legalistic jargon, the fund manager is the General Partner (GP), and the capital provider is called the Limited Partner (LP). Each LP must make large commitments to each fund – the minimum investment size is usually $1m, and often more than $5m. More recently, some classical funds have opened up to accredited investors and so offer much lower entry 'tickets' – as low as $50k, say. But to achieve sufficient diversification across such funds and your wider portfolio, it still means you have to be loaded to invest this way. To adapt the saying, *a few hundred grand here and there, and pretty soon you're talking real money.*

The curious thing about these commitments is that they are precisely that – contractual promises to invest in the future, rather than 'investments'. That's because these funds are what are known as 'blind pools'. The LPs don't know what the fund will invest in before they make the commitment.

Now here is the important part: if the barbarian fund manager returns at least 8% compound returns for the period during which the capital is actually invested (not just committed), then any profit is shared between the LP and GP on an 80/20 basis. This 8% is known as the 'hurdle rate' or the 'preferred rate of return'. If they don't reach this hurdle, the fund manager doesn't get any share of the upside at all.

All this seems like an unlikely proposal to fly in this modern world of defensive, evidence-based decision-making and sign-off by a bureaucratic committee.

But institutional investors in private markets have observed that there is something much more powerful than verification – and that's alignment. The uncertainty and opacity faced by the investors when they make the commitments are offset by the fact that profits will be shared, creating an alignment of interest. No amount of best-practice, policy or promises can compete with the effectiveness of contractually shared interests. The power of such simple partnership agreements was not discovered by abstract theorising but through experimentation and shared experiences, over vast tracts of time.

★

Following the fall of Rome in the mid-fifth century, indigenous people of the Italian mainland endured waves of invasions from barbarian hordes – Visigoths, Goths, Huns, Lombards. After a few hundred years of giving ground to this open-door immigration policy, they found themselves pushed out to the very edge of *terra firma*: the mosquito-infested marshes and lagoons of Latina Veneta in the Adriatic Sea. They survived by driving wooden piles into the mud and building out platforms to live on.

Observing the people of Venice in the 8th century CE, a dispassionate chronicler might assume that they would shortly disappear from the historical record.

Things weren't much better on the other side of the Italian boot, where the ancient port of Genoa had been overrun by a succession of Goths and then, to cap it all, was almost destroyed by Saracen pirates.

But by the start of the 12th century, both of these forlorn and unpromising communities, on the very edge of existence and keeping alive, perhaps, just the faintest spark of a lost civilisation, had become some of the most powerful maritime nations the world had ever seen – city-states and commercial republics that were hugely influential in hauling Europe from the dark ages of feudalism to a modern, market-based economy.

And the way they did that was through a commercial partnership agreement that looked astonishingly similar to today's classical closed-end private markets fund. It was called a 'commenda'.

From Resolvable to Radical Uncertainty

To take a company public and list it on the stock market is a real palaver. It takes years of preparation and an investor 'road show' that can take many months, wherein the CEO goes around the world with a team of investment bankers and a slide show, to talk to big investment groups about how the company makes its profits, why it will continue to make money and why it will grow and grow. The books are opened, presentations are given, brochures are printed, deals are struck, and then, the big day, when the top team rings the bell at the stock exchange, like the crew on an old galleon as it tries to signal something important through the fog. (Once it has launched, ordinary investors are finally able to dive in too.)

As they smash the champagne against the hull, it is a moment of great nervousness and superstition. No matter how much preparation goes into it, nobody quite knows how the whole thing will go off. It depends so much, you see, on the weather that day, the wider climate of opinion and events outside of the crew's control.

The investment bankers do what they can to stack the deck. The stock 'flotation' is set in a deliberate 'trough' so that it will rise up the crest in early trading to give it some nice early momentum. And the aim of the game – *the number one priority* – is to make sure everything about the business and its listing is presented as predictable. (Just add that old caveat about past performance, of course.) In other words, a good publicly listed company is one that is a known quantity. It shouldn't need too much work or restructuring. It shouldn't be all potential and no actuality. And once it's listed, there should be no big surprises (even if they're good ones). If all goes to plan, it's a very convenient and inclusive ownership structure.

But it's not really an investment in an enterprise – in the sense of an entrepreneurial undertaking. It is one of stewardship, which is why the executive leadership team are called 'officers'. They are appointed as administrative agents, charged with overseeing the delivery of a promise made upon the initial public offering. And this predictability is necessary because of the shareholder structure, which is now unconstrained. Anybody can take a piece of the company, and its shares can trade thousands of times a second. With no stability in its ownership structure, it is like a ship with a relentlessly disloyal crew, threatening to mutiny at every slight turn of fortune.

Public markets are great for assets offering relatively certain outcomes. This suits businesses with stable income streams. But with many stocks, what investors tend to get is the *worst* of both worlds – neither the predictability of economic performance nor the ability for the officer-stewards to manoeuvre the ship as they see fit.

This may seem a sweeping assessment of a very diverse set of public companies, but if you look closely, it only really deviates from my caricature in so far as those companies deviate from publicly listed purity, for instance by continuing to have large shareholders with effective control. Without this, various forms of cronyism tend to develop in an attempt to solve the problem.

So what is the problem? It is that the real world of enterprise and business investment is not certain. It is not calculable in advance, and this fact makes much mainstream investment theory, which assumes investment risk is quantifiable, redundant.

★

Professor John Kay and Mervyn King, a former Bank of England governor, have drawn a distinction between what they call *resolvable uncertainty* and *radical uncertainty*.[1] The resolvable type of uncertainty can be removed by looking something up (like a capital city) or applying a known probability distribution (like for coin-tossing).

By contrast, radical uncertainty is when you can't simply 'look up' the answer and there is not enough data to impute a probability. Often you will only know that you don't know what you don't know. And that's by far the most common type of uncertainty.

These days, many forms of radical uncertainty are dressed up as resolvable. That's because it's easier for middlemen to sell you optimised solutions to your problems if it looks like they have clever fixes. Examples of this include when your doctor encourages you to take drugs rather than change your diet, when a banker talks about probability rather than prudence and when investment managers talk about 'efficient' portfolios. That's because most investment is *radically* uncertain, and that's why complex investment solutions that claim to be able to 'optimise' your exposure and reduce your risk usually just disguise risk and therefore magnify it.

Instead, amid radical uncertainty, assume that any attempt to calculate or scheme your way to success will probably backfire (because this is to deploy linear solutions to non-linear problems). Rather, look at what successful solutions of the past have in common, and copy that. Often, such 'rules of thumb' will be conspicuously poorly optimised. This may be a feature not a bug, because optimisation belongs in the domain of resolvable uncertainty. Classic private markets funds are not 'optimal'. They are not whizzy financial instruments. Their value is in the constraint they impose as much as the freedom they allow.

To invest like a barbarian is a radically uncertain undertaking, because any exciting new business opportunity will often be fleeting and time-sensitive, somewhat vague and ill-defined, and have an 'unfolding' quality. Harnessing such opportunities requires both some calculation but also intuitive leaps, patience and agility, commitment and adaptability, and the outcomes can range from complete failure to outrageous success (although investing in a fund programme is nowhere near as risky as this makes things sound, as we shall see). On top of this, there is the information asymmetry, whereby the capital provider (in our case, the LP) will typically know less about the prospects of the investment than the provider of labour (in our case, the GP). And the same applies at the next level down, whereby the fund manager will know less about the company they are investing in than the entrepreneurs and managers who run it day-to-day.

There are many examples of how different cultures have dealt with the radical uncertainty of investment by the way they have brought together wealth and labour. And the approaches they adopted, over the course of centuries of trial and error, all ended up looking astonishingly similar.

The Seeding of Modern Civilisation

The first reference in medieval history to capital investment is in the will of Duke Giustiniano Parteciaco of Venice in 829, referring to ships and their goods.[2] (His name, oddly enough, is from the same root as the word 'partnership'.) Previous ancient cultures had looked upon production as a fixed quantity, and that wasn't far from the truth in as much as that production in agrarian societies was in landed property, signorial rights and ancient farming practices. But the Venetians, from their fixed-yet-floating refuge, did not look back to the plough. They turned their gaze to the horizon – to Egypt and the great port cities of Constantinople and Alexandria, the last dry-landing of silks, spices and metals from the East, before they could continue their onward journey to Europe.

Men like Parteciaco valued the enablers of trade higher than its fruits. In other words, he saw the value of capital.

But such investments were risky. The voyages were long, fraught with danger and they were expensive, requiring large crews to man galleys on expeditions that lasted many months, or longer, should they have to winter abroad. Only the wealthiest could afford to fund such trips, and even for them, the risk was great.

One approach to financing such voyages was to use the Roman *foenus nauticum* or 'sea loans', with fixed rates of interest. These had the benefit of simplicity. But from the investor's perspective, if the venture was a great success, they would still only get their fixed return, despite the high risk of losing their principal entirely. From the merchant's perspective, if it was successful, that was good for him, but if business was difficult, he still had to pay back the loan.[3]

But in the mid-10th century, Venetian traders and investors adopted a different arrangement: the commenda. The word essentially meant 'trust', and this partnership quickly became the dominant investment vehicle. Within a few decades, the city began to dominate trade in the Asiatic and by the end of the 11th century had secured major trading privileges with Byzantium and 'most favoured nation' status in the empire, eclipsing its rivals and making it the main trading hub of the Mediterranean basin, connecting West to East.[4]

The essential features of the commenda were strikingly similar to those of the modern private markets fund.[5]

There was a stay-at-home capital investor, which was called the 'commendator' ('one who entrusts' – this is the LP).

Then, there was the sea-faring merchant and provider of labour, which was called the tractator (from the same root as the word 'transact' – our 'GP' or fund manager).

Between them, there is a profit-sharing arrangement, just as in modern closed-end funds. Almost invariably across the ancient world, the split was on a 75/25 basis in the investors' favour. Invariably in the modern private markets fund, the split is slightly more in the investor's favour, at 80/20. Perhaps the extra 5% was danger money. The commendator was typically obliged to cover the cost of burial, should the merchant die mid-voyage.

Typically, the merchant fronts a share of the capital to ensure 'skin in the game' or 'alignment of interests', which is also the case with modern versions. And also in line with today, commenda agreements limited the liability of the commendator to the capital they invested. Without this, a merchant could have made a whole family bankrupt and thus become ostracised from Venetian society.

The commenda was also limited by duration – i.e. closed-ended. It would apply for just one voyage (in this case, a literal voyage!) and this ensured the investor gets their money back and realises their profits (not merely an accounting or booked profit) so that they then have the option to reinvest in the merchant's next venture (or the GP's next fund) or to decline to do so. On the flip side, this finite term of both the commenda and limited partnership means the merchant is highly motivated to perform well, otherwise they will not be able to raise funds for future ventures.

Typically, ships would travel in convoys, mimicking how modern private markets funds invest in a dozen or so companies to diversify risk.

Meanwhile, upstream, the wealthy Venetians would finance dozens of such ventures at any one time, just as a modern institutional investor will today be an investor in multiple funds, to diversify their risk.

The cynic might say this looks merely like an interesting historical coincidence. But while Western scholars have tended to focus on the commenda, the essential features of this partnership are present in trading agreements across a wide variety of cultures for the best part of a thousand years.

Examples that pre-date even the Commenda include the Roman *societas* (or 'partnership') of labour and capital, which saw the merchant invest alongside the capital provider for 'skin in the game'. The Jewish 'isqa' contract (a Talmudic term that survives in modern Hebrew as 'esek' or 'business') attempted to align capital and labour in a way that sidestepped usury – this was more a semi-loan, semi-trust, and over time, the fixed liability on the part of the merchant appears to have softened. Indeed, in some markets, Jewish traders preferred the *qirad*, an Islamic partnership agreement wherein the merchant was not liable for the loss of any part of the investor's capital.

Such was the popularity of the qirad that it came to be used in maritime trade all over the Indian Ocean. But originally, the qirad (which meant to 'share' [profits]) was used to finance caravan trade across the Arabian deserts, and it involved, again, a 25/75 split between the travelling merchant and the stay-at-home investor.

Islam Seeded by Venture Capital

One rather successful qirad investor was named Khadijah, a widow and one of the wealthiest and most respected merchants in pre-Islamic Arabia. She managed a large trading enterprise and used qirad agreements with travelling merchants to invest her capital in long-range caravan expeditions, trading silk, spices, precious metals and grain. One such merchant is said to have delivered an unusually high rate of return on a venture to Syria, doubling Khadijah's investment capital, and consequently doing well for himself too. His name was Muhammed, and Khadijah was sufficiently impressed by his business acumen and fair dealing in the partnership that she agreed to marriage. She later became the first convert to Islam and it is widely acknowledged in early Islamic histories that the profits from her ventures were essential for supporting her husband's rise and in nurturing the emergent Muslim religion.

Academics debate about which of these contracts came first, and whether or not they are, in fact, direct forebears of the modern private markets fund. The important point for us is that solutions that map so closely to today's vehicles were ubiquitous across the ancient world, to the extent that, to trace their history gives us 'the historiography of commercial law' itself.[6] Modern private markets are no 'flash in the pan', they are the inheritors of a system that gave rise to the Doges of Venice, to world-changing religions and to the modern Western world of free exchange.

*

It is difficult to avoid the conclusion that the reason these agreements are so similar (to each other and the modern private markets) is because they evolved, through long, cross-cultural trial-and-error, to solve similar problems, presented by similar situations.

Like its ancient antecedents, the modern private markets fund offers an elegant solution that aligns the interests of investor and manager. It ensures that both parties have exposure to both the upside and the downside – essential, given that the risk and reward cannot be predicted or calculated in advance.

This exposure is equitable, so each party only risks what they put in: there is no liability on the part of the manager to compensate the investor if the venture fails, and no obligation on the part of the investor to compensate the manager, should he take on debts, above and beyond the original capital commitment. And likewise, each party would receive profits in proportion to what they put in.

Given this strongly aligned interest, the investor can afford to give away his right (and ability) to control his investment during the life of the venture. He entrusts day-to-day decisions to the manager, who is best placed to make such decisions. This in turn gives the manager the necessary agility, time and initiative to take advantage of emergent opportunities. (Contrast a modern stock-market investment, where the shareholder has 'transparency' and regulated reporting about the asset but must put blind faith in the company officers to manage it well on his behalf. LPs that invest in a blind pool have no such transparency but can be confident that their interests will be served, though the merchant sails far beyond the horizon to do so.[i])

The finite lifespan of these agreements also meant there was a perpetual need to recommit – meaning that no amount of apathy would have seen the commenda endure. This leads to another conclusion: the commenda agreements were considered sufficiently profitable, equitable and worthwhile for our wealthy forebears to pursue, repeatedly, for centuries.

It would be so much *easier* if these funds just lived forever (or until they are run into the ground, go bust or are acquired by a bigger fish), as is the case for listed companies or mutual funds. This would also mean profits could be reinvested within the same vehicle, creating measurable compound returns. This would enable analysts to make nice graphs of a manager's long-term performance, and then they could compare that with Berkshire Hathaway and public market funds. Meanwhile, the top people at the fund management firm wouldn't have to spend six months every few years raising fresh funds.

But when you have to return all your investors' money and wind up the whole enterprise, it keeps the manager very honest and very focused. One bad fund, one breach of trust, and they may never raise another. Meanwhile, the investor buys a real cash flow asset. They put money in. They get (hopefully much more) money back.

★

---

[i] Because of the times and the entrepreneurial nature of those early maritime nations, the line between economic activity, nation-building and foreign affairs was rather blurred. As a result, the phenomenal organising power of the commenda made it as much an instrument of state as private wealth creation. For instance, Enrico Dandolo, Doge of Venice (1192–1205) used commenda agreements to organise massive fleets of traders and sailors for the Fourth Crusade, which he led, funded by wealthy Venetians and sailing under the Venetian banner. Some historians even argue that the decision to divert the Fourth Crusade to Constantinople was influenced by the commercial interests of the commenda. In a reversal of this, a purely commercial commenda was subverted, at least once, for state-building. In the wake of the First Crusade, two of Genoa's most successful privateers, the Embriaco Brothers, raised commenda investments from the city's wealthy patrons and used them to establish trading posts in the new Crusader States along the coast of North Africa in an attempt to dominate the timber trade, essential for shipbuilding and therefore the enablement of commerce itself. Think of it as Medieval Apple Pay. It all went to plan, but, rather than return their investor's capital and profits immediately, the brothers then sailed east and reinvested the capital to corner the markets in cedar and pine. They built fortresses to protect their investments and – perhaps this is the point at which success may have gone to their heads – rather than returning to share the profits in Genoa, they declared themselves independent lords and heads of state in their new territories. They became rulers of dynasties that lasted another two centuries. The closed-ended incentive mechanism that forces the GP to return capital in order to raise ever larger funds does not hold if they can literally crown themselves kings (not just Kings of Capital!).

At first, such commenda agreements were the preserve of the wealthy, just as the modern private markets fund has long been the preserve of institutions and the very rich, with minimum investment sizes in the millions of dollars. But over time, even those of more modest means, such as Venetian nuns and notaries, Genoese artisans and widows, Montepellian blacksmiths, dyers and masons, even apprentices, began to invest small sums in larger commenda in order to benefit from an emerging international market. This is precisely the same evolutionary path of the modern private markets fund, and the reason for this book.

From the exercise of commerce and trade, the maritime nations of the medieval ages realised that they could create new wealth and put riches within reach of the city's humblest citizen, through their participation in *commenda* – a structure that became as familiar to these societies as stock-market trading is to our own – and probably more so.

These agreements crossed cultural and religious barriers and led directly to the development of the modern free market and the globalisation of trade. Commenda-style merchants, whether Christian, Muslim or Jew, became the first cosmopolitans, and in so doing, lifted their own communities out of the Malthusian cycle of zero-sum over- and under-production that faced agrarian societies throughout countless ages and into a world of commerce, exchange and prosperity.

So much for barbarians.

★

Seen from space, the light pollution from Europe maps neatly onto affluent centres across the former Roman empire, as do the road networks. There is even demonstrably better mental health among modern populations living today just within the borders of what was the Roman empire than those just outside it.[7] In our world of hyper-novelty and technological change, we tend to underrate the impact of the past.

So on balance, the idea that an investment agreement that was ubiquitous across the ancient and medieval world could have vanished out of all memory and usage, but was then repeatedly reinvented, seems less likely to me than that of a real connection between these ancient investment agreements and today's private markets vehicles. A historian would need evidence of such a continuum, but these vehicles are not usually enshrined in legislation; they are evolved behaviours, passed down through the practice of pragmatic commercial law, from scribes to notaries to lawyers, via nudges and tips and winks and the dusting off of memories and ledgers.

Eventually, though, the commenda is thought to have been translated into the Napoleonic Commercial Code of 1807, the modern version of which gives us the French private markets fund.

But for several centuries, this partnership and profit-sharing approach to venturing, prospecting and investment fell from regular usage, perhaps as the genteel world of the 19th century appeared to be less radically uncertain than the past, and the wealthy began to 'appreciate' the value of what they knew more than the opportunities that lay beyond the horizon.

But commenda-style partnership agreements never fully go away – they bubble up whenever opportunities, risks and information-asymmetries collide. One example was the American oil rush of the late 1800s.

The father of the petroleum industry, Edwin L Drake, burnt through his life savings of $200 and then a loan of $500 and then investor funds of $3,000, before he struck black gold beside a stream in Titusville, Pennsylvania, and became the first person to commercialise oil production through mechanical drilling techniques.[8] But he failed to benefit commercially from his great discovery and faced financial difficulties through to his death in 1880. But it wasn't long before the oil business had its first billionaire, in John D Rockefeller. Rockefeller didn't use savings, loans and desperate appeals in order to fund his ascent. He developed informal partnerships with sedentary and silent investors, before forming Standard Oil, which was legally a corporation but in practice functioned like a privately owned partnership with tight control and passive investors who had little to no role in governance.

However, the first oil company recorded to have habitually used limited partnership agreements (the legal form of private market funds used in much of the Anglosphere) was Apache Oil, set up in the 1950s and which is now a Nasdaq listed company. In response to the high risks and sharp practices of many prospectors, the firm built its business using a succession of partnerships that allowed investors to spread risk over multiple drilling sites. Such was its success that by 1961, Apache had diversified into private real estate limited partnerships and opened up 'a 50-store shopping plaza in suburban Minneapolis with the help of 13 mayors, 12 beauty queens and a 60-piece marching band'.[9]

The Dawn of Modern Private Markets

In the spirit of boundless optimism and an appreciation for the power of science that characterised America following the Second World War, various financially astute ex-soldiers started experimenting with mechanisms that would help channel investment into commercial innovation.

One of these was William Henry Draper Jr. He had been an Army General, leading a division that fought on the Western Front, before becoming chief of the Economics Division of the post-war Allied Control Council for Germany, where he advocated free market policies for the rehabilitation of German economic (and military) power in the face of the crony capitalist propaganda programme known as the Marshall Plan. In 1959, he joined forces with Rowan Gaither, the founder of the RAND Corporation, and Frederick Anderson, who had run the 8th Bomber Command from London that conducted daring daylight bombing raids over Berlin.

Together, the trio decided to set up a company in a sleepy West Coast town surrounded by an abundance of apricot orchards, near an air force base they happened to know.[10] It was called Paolo Alto but today it's better known as Silicon Valley. Their firm, Draper, Gaither & Anderson, initially described itself as a 'special situations' firm – a phrase with a militaristic ring. But they soon replaced it with the less cryptic 'venture capital'. The firm raised a $6m LP fund, with a ten-year life, and an 80/20 profit-share between investors and managers.

Thus, it was that modern private markets, as they exist today, sprang into existence, in the form of the first private markets 'venture capital' LP fund.

In an age that had mobilised whole societies in two total wars in the space of 30 years, taxation had now become a major consideration for any investor, and an activity that involved one company buying another would tend to attract a double layer of taxation. The limited partnership structure neatly sidestepped this and allowed the venture capital managers to treat their share of any profits, not as income, but to be taxed once, as capital gains. This proved to be another major – and controversial – attraction of the vehicle in the decades ahead.

The venture capital exploits of William Draper, the 'Wall Street General', are barely a footnote on his Wikipedia page, but the Draper name continues to be one of the biggest in venture capital. More to the point, he set the standard for the limited partnership model that was subsequently adopted by every major venture capital firm the world over, before being adopted, a few decades later, by a trillion-dollar private capital industry.

★

Twenty-five years later and 8,000 miles across the Atlantic, Jonathan Blake was the next in a millennium-long line of lawyers, notaries and clerks, who was tipped a wink and nudged in the direction of a well-adapted profit-sharing partnership between capital and labour.

It was 1982, and he was a lawyer working for a start-up law firm called SJ Berwin. And he was sitting in a meeting with a client who was interested in setting up a venture capital fund. The client had a number of requirements that were unusual. In particular, he wanted his fund to be onshore, which generally meant it would get double taxed whenever it tried to sell a business. Halfway through the meeting, Jonathan's boss, Stanley Berwin, popped his head in, and when Jonathan explained the client's unusual requests, his boss said 'why not use a limited partnership'.

'I'd never heard of a limited partnership', recalls Jonathan. 'They were just a footnote in the textbooks at university. I thought it was a stupid idea, but I didn't dare question him'.

It seems hard to believe now, but lawyers working in London's investment banking market had little to no idea of the private markets fund structures that had begun to be used in California decades before, and that had become such a fertile source of technological innovation and business creation. As far as this young lawyer knew, limited partnerships hadn't been used anywhere before, outside of farming.

He spent the next few weeks creaking open dusty old books and trying to work out how to apply the vehicle to venture capital and how to make it efficient.

Today, Jonathan Blake is considered the father of the modern private equity industry in Europe. The terms of that first £2m European private markets limited partnership fund were, of course, an 80/20 profit-share.

★

In the sweep of history, modern private markets look a lot more like classical investment than today's high-tech, high-frequency, algorithmic, statistical, regulated, highly liquid public markets trading. We may be more familiar with stock markets but make no mistake – it is the newcomer. By contrast, private markets type structures are time-tested, naturally selected, well-adapted solutions that tend to bring wealth and prosperity wherever they are put to work.

Given the provenance of private-markets style partnerships, the big question might actually be why such structures aren't a much more common way of doing business today. One line of thinking (that I find plausible) is that, as societies become more protectionist, defensive, centralised and bureaucratic, they tend towards economic structures that extract value, particularly through debt and interest mechanisms. While profit-sharing is more logical for market participants, such as merchants dealing with other merchants, it requires a certain level of trust and cooperation between the two parties. A hierarchical creditor–debtor arrangement is simpler to enforce and therefore preferred by bureaucracies that value theoretical certainty over the opportunities presented by risk-taking, profit-sharing and investment in potential.[11]

Indeed, the fall of Venice from maritime superpower to sinking museum-town has been attributed to illiberal, centralising moves by the Venetian elite in the early 14th century. One of the first lurches towards extractive economic institutions was to ban commenda contracts, an obvious target for those willing to sacrifice upward social mobility and economic dynamism on the altar of nationalist protectionism. By the year 1500, the population of Venice had shrunk to one hundred thousand, and as the European population grew in the following centuries, Venice stagnated and shrank.[12]

'There is no remembrance of former things', says the Book of Ecclesiastes. 'There is no new thing under the sun'. Private markets aren't an invention. They sit timelessly, and with an astonishing degree of homogeneity, within the logic of human experience and cooperation. They have been discovered, and cast aside and rediscovered, over the course of a millennium or more.

That's why I look on private markets with the wonder of Shakespeare's Miranda and, at the same time, with the weariness of her father, Prospero, the powerful magician usurped from his rightful place as Duke of Milan. On the one hand, we have this shining inheritance, plain to see (if you look back far enough): an equitable profit-sharing arrangement with magical power – the power to realise potential, encourage greater cooperation between diverse cultures and bring forth prosperity. On the other, there is a siren call, an undercurrent of fear, tugging us back to our shoreline – the eternal impulse to sacrifice potential on the altar of certainty. As if that will save us from the storm.

For insight into the origins of private markets, scan this QR code.

2

The Enemy Within

'I am the punishment of God. . . If you had not committed great sins, God would not have sent a punishment like me upon you'.
— **Genghis Khan**

Today, public and private markets look like opposites. But they are not light versus day — they are more like denominations of the same religion that started in the same place, and through a few differing interpretations, ended up widely divergent.

Public market governance started to diverge from the interests of beneficial owners more than a century ago. The classic critique of corporate governance in public markets was written in 1932. In it, Adolf Berle and Gardiner Means tried to characterise how a 'public' company was typically run about a hundred years before that, i.e. in the 1830s. They had the impression of a group of owners who delegated powers to managers and who were strictly accountable to those owners.

> They occupied, in fact, a position analogous to that of the captain and officers of a ship at sea, in navigation their autonomy might be supreme; but the direction of the voyage, the alteration of the vessel, the character of the cargo, and the distribution of the profits and losses were settled ahead of time and altered only by the [the owners].[1]

If you didn't know, you would think they were describing a modern private markets partnership. But in the pursuit of scale and efficiency, this disconnection between owner and agent has steadily grown for stock market listed companies.[2]

In fact, this problem – where managers are not closely accountable to the owners of companies – was flagged much earlier. Adam Smith, writing about joint-stock companies in the late 18th century, pointed out something that has come to be known as the principal-agent problem, or simply, 'the agency problem'. He noted the directors of companies being 'the managers of other people's money' are less likely to watch over it with the same 'anxious vigilance' as if it were their own. In this conception, today's stock market would be appropriate for companies where 'the operations are capable of being reduced to the routine', such as banking, insurance, canal navigation, and to which we might add infrastructure like toll roads, airports and utilities.[3] In other words, the stock exchange would be a market for buying the right to passive interest that requires oversight but not managerial brilliance.

By the early 20th century, companies listed on the stock exchange were many and varied, and getting ever larger. They were also owned by an ever-greater number of shareholders, who took ever-smaller stakes in each company, and therefore had less and less say over how the business was run – to the point where, as Berle and Means declared: 'The owners of passive property have surrendered the power of control, and actual control has passed to the managers'.

Later commentators referred to the propensity of company managers to 'shirk' and 'steal' from investors, with the latter referring to excessive perks and pay. And by the early 1970s, this propensity had become endemic. The many excesses of corporate executives prompted two more academics, Michael Jensen and Bill Meckling, to pick up where Adam Smith left off, and point towards the minimal equity ownership of managers who run companies as a potential weakness in corporate governance. In an academic paper in 1976, they combined such 'agency' theory with capital structure theory and posited the fantastical notion that it might be more efficient for managers to use debt to buy back 99% of the public stock, and hold a 1% equity stake for themselves, thereby realign ownership and control.[4] To worshippers of the Market the prospect was anathema. But a few maverick investment bankers saw the logic, and began to formulate a way to rescue bloated, badly run listed companies – by taking them private.

★

Private equity is often associated with the leveraged buyout or 'LBO', since this is the method private equity firms typically use to buy companies – and it was the spark-plug for today's giant private markets industry.

An LBO is similar to buying a house with a mortgage, and a private equity firm is similar to someone who repeatedly buys houses, improves them and sells them for a profit. Just, instead of a house, it's a company and instead of calling it a mortgage, it's called leverage. And that's pretty much the whole deal. Compared to most modern financial chicanery, the essence of a private equity backed LBO is incredibly simple. And yet when the LBO came along, it took corporate America by total surprise, subverting the status quo and throwing the establishment-elite into such a state of indignation and uproar that they have never fully recovered.

LBOs are the wheelie suitcase of corporate finance. People were familiar with wheels and suitcases for a long time before anyone thought to combine the two. Back in the 1970s, everyone had to carry their luggage. Well, not the CEOs of big businesses. They had bag-carriers and motorcades. And they presided over other things so massive they thought nobody could carry them off: namely, the bloated conglomerates that they managed. And because they thought nobody could lift them out of the public markets, they were managed less like enterprises designed to provide their shareholders with a good return, and more like private empires run for the benefit of their management-stewards.

It amounted to a corporate obesity epidemic, a cultural psychopathology that had been decades in the making. Since the Great Depression, a generation of company-men had learned that small was not beautiful and that the economy could move against you indefinitely. As a result, they saw their job less as providing long-term value to shareholders and more as building companies that were so big they couldn't fail.

Given their atomised shareholder base, investors had very little say over the running of these companies. The slave with two masters is a freeman, so they say. *The slave with a hundred thousand is more like an emperor.* And so naturally, these managers began to empire-build: precisely as the academics of decades and centuries before, predicted.

To be fair, it is difficult to even conceptualise so many masters without resorting to some form of abstraction. And the abstraction that CEOs adopted was that of the Market. They observed how the Market seemed to behave and they adapted their own behaviour accordingly. They noticed that the predictability of earnings was greeted favourably and was preferred even to unexpectedly good news. So these corporate-stewards would run the conglomerates in an ultra-conservative manner: very low debt levels, lots of cash, extreme diversification into businesses that were entirely unrelated to their current activities, but with very little in the way of genuine R&D investments, meanwhile paying themselves handsomely. Their jobs would be safe and the huge amount of excess cash could be soaked up by prestige-investments such as fleets of private jets and assistants to assistants. They also deployed their own form of bogus leverage, where the companies they bought up would be valued higher than previously, merely by virtue of being part of their mothership.

Back on main street, there were signs that something was rotten in the capitalist system. In the 1970s, New York City was like the picture of Dorian Gray – a crime-ridden, mafia-infested, cesspool of corruption. In 1975, it only avoided bankruptcy via a federal bailout, as middle-class residents began fleeing to the suburbs. The once-proud gateway to the land of opportunity was now managed for the benefit of a corporate elite at the expense of its citizens and shareholders. It was also a function of a Faustian pact between big business and policymakers. Decades of protectionist industrial policy designed to protect American corporate interests had resulted in a massive misallocation of capital, while wage and price controls and central bank monetary manipulation during the 1960s, had finally given way to stagflation (this is normally all blamed on an 'oil price shock'). The economy was tanking and corporate profits were in free fall.

At last, America's investors decided the conglomerate model was broken and in October 1975, they began to sell out. The S&P 500 fell to almost half its peak of two years before.

But the CEOs were not quick to respond to this message from investors, because they had built large defences around their own positions. They had recently formed a powerful lobby cooperative; they had peopled their boards with acolytes; and the legislature was also on their side (and as we will see, that is still the case to a degree). While the share price carnage prompted some to sell off non-core divisions, these were discreet affairs between peers. What was needed was something even more drastic than a stock market crash to shock the system of corporate control and patronage into submission and bring the 'mad men' era to an end.

*

Any good banker knows that prestige is more important than money, and back in the mid-20th century, there were two types of banking: grubby money-lending and *haute finance*. What Jerome Kohlberg had going in the proverbial basement of Bear Stearns was definitely not high finance. Kohlberg led the banks' so-called 'bootstrap' deals – buyouts of corporate orphans (unloved divisions of the increasingly forlorn conglomerates), and on a very small-scale – in the single digit millions of dollars. The bank's leadership team were not keen on this activity and they refused to unleash the power of these deals to solve the great problem of the age – the lack of corporate control by the owners of capital. So Kohlberg hired two relatives, George Roberts and his cousin Henry Kravis, both in their 30s, and together they spun out to form Kohlberg, Kravis, Roberts, today called KKR.

Their plan was simple: they would apply these bootstrapping techniques, not just to corporate orphans, but, eventually, to the conglomerates themselves, and they could do this by using the company they were going to buy as collateral to raise debt to fund the purchase, just like buying a house with a mortgage. But this was even better, because you have to repay a mortgage from your salary. You can repay an LBO from the cash flow of the company you are buying (since it is a productive, cash-generating asset).

In 1976, their first year of independent operation as Kohlberg Kravis Roberts, they pulled off their first LBO, backed by a small group of insurance companies and bankers. It received little public attention. But three years later, they did another, much bigger deal: the $355 m take-private of Houdaille Industries. This time, Wall Street went apoplectic. *How had they done it?* Every banker wanted to get their hands on the legal documents to find out how it was done. Suddenly, the floodgates were open. The barbarians had arrived.

At first, these buyout shops, of which there were just a couple of others emerging in the mid-1970s, had to accept debt at very high rates of interest from insurance companies. But they weren't the only fringe players subverting the world of mainstream finance. A young banker named Michael Milken, based in a suburban branch of a second-tier investment bank, Drexel Burnham, had figured out a way to sell debt to finance smaller companies than the mainstream bond market would have dreamed of servicing. Milken's 'junk bond' investors turned out to be the perfect market to soak up the surging demand for leveraged buyout debt – a forerunner to the much larger private credit market that is only today fully emerging.

Such was the conservative cash position of these target businesses that several early buyouts were done with virtually no equity at all. They were just using the stuff the company owned as collateral for the bonds to buy the company.

It is difficult to overstate the unsettling nature of this situation for incumbents. Suddenly, a couple of unknown-upstarts, backed by grubby money provided by fringe 'junk' bond lenders, could acquire massive, listed companies and take them private, decapitate the leadership team and the profligate company headquarters. It was an undermining of the corporate establishment that was so effective that it reshaped corporate America in a fundamental way – from cronyism and waste to efficiency and growth. For this, they have never been fully forgiven.

While the LBO was a simple idea, it was also a revelation so shocking that, to this day, people are still debating it. Many of these buyout firms are now the biggest power brokers on Wall Street, but their sins can still not be washed away. No matter how big private equity gets, it will always be a corporate revolutionary, because that's its *raison d'être*. After all, they are barbarians, remember?

In popular culture, the 1980s were a 'greed-is-good' raid on corporate America. Men in red braces shouting into a bulky mobile phone to break up a company and sell the pieces. Had these original corporate raiders and buyout boys been as concerned with public relations as their modern successors, they might have tried to frame things differently. They might have issued a press release to say they were on a mission to Make Corporate America Great Again.

By Odin, did they succeed.

*

I said at the start that public and private markets are not 'opposites', but you might think that all this certainly seems antagonistic, even aggressive: like a lion taking down a zebra. But if you've seen the *Lion King*, you'll know it's just part of the symbiotic circle of life. In fact, it should be even less antagonistic than that: private equity isn't a predator at all. It's more like a rehab clinic for celebrities.

Celebrities live in the public spotlight – they can't just be independent 'artists' – their whole lives are permeated by the incessant glare of fame and public interest, and they have a duty to stay on-brand, to do interviews, to market their films, albums (increasingly, their own venture capital funds – that's another story). But there comes a point when they can no longer be productive in this intensely public arena. Maybe they get flabby and need a diet of kale, or maybe they need to bulk up for some superhero movie and spend a few months eating wagyu (OK, I won't push the analogy too far). But the point is, rehab is temporary.

Just as all roads once led to Rome, ultimately everything eventually comes back round to the public markets. In the final analysis, private markets managers end up wrapping back towards them, whether to achieve liquidity for their companies, their investors or themselves. And likewise, without private markets, public markets do not have the governance mechanisms to self-correct. They need each other.

With the emergence of LBOs in the late 1970s, the stock exchange model of corporate ownership now faced precisely this healthy competition in the market for control of big corporations from private markets investors – and a corrective for those companies that needed rehab therapy.

Such is the importance of this symbiosis that the economist and author Donald Chew has attributed this battle for corporate control to a renaissance that ushered in a golden age for corporate America, which has seen an average of 12% returns from US stock markets for four decades.

It is worth considering that private equity can take some real credit, not only for its own performance, but also for that of public markets, which, by its mere existence, it keeps on the straight and narrow.

*

Back in 2012, Dell Computers was a listed company in dire need of some 'me-time'. The computer and laptop maker looked like an artefact, a once-great company, written off by the stock markets and soon to fall victim to the creative destruction of technological progress that it had once led. (Asian manufacturers had led a race to the bottom in laptops, while Apple had shifted the market towards tablets.) Its revenues had stagnated for years previously, and in its final quarter as a public company, income plummeted by more than 70%.

What happened next was one of the most remarkable acts of corporate rehabilitation, wealth creation and personal come-backs in business history – and it was all achieved with the private equity playbook.

In a 2021 piece, Forbes called the $25 billion buyout in 2013 the 'Deal of the Century'.[5] It remains the largest technology LBO ever, and it is revealing in many ways – not least because it had little to do with the mainstream buyout industry. In this case, the master of the universe, frontline barbarian and buyout raider was not a private equity professional at all. He was a nerdy, affable man with thick glasses and a penchant for taking computers apart and putting them back together again better. It was Michael Dell himself.

Michael Dell teamed up with a tech focused private equity fund (that he was also an investor in) called Silver Lake. When they re-listed the businesses five years later, they looked very different and were worth four times as much, approximately $70 billion. The investment propelled Dell from rapidly falling tech star to the 14th richest person on earth – he personally netted about $40 billion.

Even at the time, the buyout was highly controversial. Michael Dell owned 15% of the listed company prior to the buyout, and although he was not allowed to vote, the management and board all favoured a delisting, which prompted some to call it 'an inside job'. And it was. The insiders knew and understood the company's potential. As much as they tried, the Market refused to see it. The company had pivoted towards the fast-growing enterprise technology and data management market and it had huge potential that just wasn't recognised by the stock markets, and it could not therefore capitalise on those opportunities with an ownership base that didn't 'get it'.

And that was the problem. It desperately needed some private time. It needed to go into rehab.

Nine Out of 10 CEOs Prefer Private Equity

The symbiotic relationship I have so far described between public and private markets is an ideal – how, over the long term, things should work. A public market kept healthy by periodic take-privates, which after a time return to the market in an 'initial public offering'. But encroaching rules and regulations, combined with ever more passive shareholders, have convinced more and more celebrity entrepreneurs and business owners to want to stay in permanent rehab. It's a phenomenon referred to as 'staying private for longer'.

The stock markets used to be full of glamour, and a main market listing was a source of kudos and credibility, helping to attract big customers and coverage. But a seemingly perpetual increase in regulation, bureaucracy and intermediation has resulted in an exodus of talent from the public markets. Given that regulatory regimes differ across borders, the situation can be more or less extreme (the UK, for example, is notably bad), but it is not great anywhere.

There will always be more regulatory burden for listed companies, that's part of the deal. The question is whether it's worth it. For much of the 20th century, the deal was clearly worth it. But in the past few decades, that bargain has soured.

Speaking in 2025, Jamie Dimon, the boss of JP Morgan, summed up the situation like this: 'We used to have a very active small IPO business. But if you're a small business – say you make a hundred million of profits and you might be worth $1.5bn – the cost of registering, the litigation, the disclosure requirements, the cookie-cutter board, [. . .] the compensation requirements, the press loves to beat up companies. . .' And that's a guy selling public listing services. (He was also heavily instrumental in making the Dell buyout happen, and maybe there is a lesson there: always be on both sides of a trade.)

The salient point for investors is that the stock market pond is shrinking, while the private seas are rising – and this is a multi-decade trend. The 'stagnation' in the number of public companies is much reported, but the figures vastly underplay the reality. If you strip out all the holding vehicles, ETFs and listed funds, the number of actual operating companies traded on US stock markets has halved since the 1990s, from about 8,000 to less than 4,000. Worse, stock markets have never been more concentrated, with the largest 10 US companies making up more than a fifth of the whole market.

Today, just 100 companies account for 80% of the trading volume on the New York Stock Exchange.

In the words of Leonard Cohen, *everybody knows the boat is leaking*. And everybody knows why. There is a powerful undercurrent that is drawing all the best companies away from public ownership, and it is called private equity.

By contrast, nine out of 10 US companies with revenues above $100m are now private, according to S&P Capital IQ. The number of private equity backed companies in the US has grown from about 2,000 in the year 2000 to more than 11,500 today. If you include venture backed companies (and why wouldn't you) it's above 60,000.

You can ignore everything else in this book, but ignore this fact, and you risk being the last day-fisherman at the side of a tepid pond where a few big fish have swallowed the rest.

The financial establishment is not happy about this but they aren't helping themselves. Instead of trying to enact change in the interests of the end-investor, many public markets players and intermediaries have adopted something of a siege mentality – flinging wild accusations about buyout firms in order to denigrate and deter them, rather than working to put their own house in order. To some degree, it has worked – buyout firms are much more wary of take-privates than they once were and it is partly because of this reputational risk, and partly because, over time, the stock markets have become so much less relevant for them as sources of deal flow.

★

After the de-listing of Dell, its new private equity owners faced a lawsuit for supposedly buying it on the cheap. The plaintiffs were activist funds, several of which had only bought shares in the company *after* Dell had announced his intended buy out. (One of the funds even had to pull out during the trial, when it emerged they had actually voted *in favour* of the buyout.) And Dell paid a 37% premium to the market price.[6] There was also a competitive process – Blackstone was invited to bid – but in the end, nobody else wanted the company, nobody else valued it.

So in desperation, the public market intermediaries turned to the weapon beloved of all extractive bureaucracies – the courts. You might think they would have no case at all, but rather than observe the 'efficient market' principles upon which the public markets are based, the Delaware judge devised his own discounted cash flow model and determined that the sale price actually undervalued the company by $7 billion.

One justification for this was that the price paid was not 'fair' because Silver Lake was not a strategic bidder but a financial buyer. Another was that stock market 'myopia' meant the share price did not reflect fair value because of investors' fixation on short-term profits.

Eventually, the Supreme Court overruled these lower court manoeuvrings and found in favour of the buyers, noting that the claims were incompatible with the efficient markets hypothesis and there was 'a deep and actively traded public float, coverage by over 30 equity analysts, evidence that the market price responded quickly to new information and no controlling stockholder'.[7]

There is no greater indication that you are on the right track than when your detractors must contravene basic logic to attack you. Nobody will ever thank these barbarians for keeping the public market healthy, and that's fine. A successful buyout is, literally, its own reward. Just ask Michael Dell.

★

The biggest losers from this defensive mentality are public market shareholders. When a private equity firm delists a company and takes it private, the average price it pays is more than 40% higher than the 'undisturbed' share price.[8] There is even an entire industry of 'activist' hedge funds that make their fortunes by doing nothing other than waiting around for buyout bids, pouncing and then complaining (and suing) when the premium the private equity firm pays isn't high enough for their tastes.

Public market intermediaries should be delighted whenever a private equity firm shows interest in a listed target – but they aren't. That could be because their interests just aren't aligned with the end-investors they represent. And it could also be because they are increasingly concerned that, once gone, the company might never come back, a process that perpetually reduces their relevance.

*

Dell did come back to market, and when it did, it had much more to offer. It had been transformed into a massive data infrastructure company. Following the buyout, Dell and his private equity sidekick at Silver Lake pulled off another coup. Having bought a company that the market had effectively written off as the next Betamax/Blackberry, they sealed a colossal 'bolt-on' deal with the $67 billion acquisition of IT infrastructure giant EMC, a company much larger than the one they had just taken-private.

While everybody was looking at Google, Amazon and Microsoft, Dell amassed a leading position in the massive market for enterprise technology, just as businesses were in the process of digitising and moving to the cloud. Some might argue that they could have pulled this off in the full glare of public market scrutiny and scepticism, but the facts of the case don't support this.

*

Being misunderstood by the market is not a happy place to be (and this can happen for many reasons) – and it is *bound* to happen to some companies – perhaps all companies – periodically. The more systemic problem is the neglect of those that are neither big nor very fast growing (a self-fulfilling prophecy if your main market for capital doesn't 'get you'). If you just have a healthy profitable business with lots of potential that is not en vogue or easy to explain, then analysts will ignore you and you will suffer the worst of both worlds: ownership that is open to unconstrained public trading and speculation while being effectively invisible.

There are many such zombie companies, unable to raise the capital they need to achieve their potential and unable to attract dynamic board members because public company governance is mainly box-ticking and back-covering. There is not even much kudos to being a listed company anymore to compensate for these constraints. The CEOs spend their time reporting to a faceless shareholder register. And their pay packet will be benchmarked and sanctioned by a remuneration committee, then published for everyone to read.

Compare this to working in a private equity owned company. You will have one set of owners, who will be sophisticated and engaged. They will share your vision and your plan and they will have the financial resources to make them a reality. It is little wonder, therefore, that so many aspirational business managers are choosing private equity.

You might think, this all sounds a very long way from RJR Nabisco style conglomerate take-downs, and you would be right. That buy-and-break strategy served a purpose at a moment in time, but it was fleeting. By the late 1980s, most buyout deals were not hostile but were formulated in cooperation with the existing management. If you are just going to break up a business and sell the parts, the existing management team isn't that consequential. But if you want to buy a business and grow it, then the people running the show are absolutely critical (private equity managers may be very engaged owners and board directors, but this is a very far cry from running a company).

During the second great buyout boom of the mid-2000s, even managers of large listed businesses started publicly expressing their wish to be bought out by private equity firms. (At Davos, shortly before the GFC, one Fortune 500 CEO begged Stephen Schwarzman, the boss of private equity group Blackstone: 'If you can do me, do me'.) It's slightly cringeworthy, but the point is this: most aspirational managers in any size of business will choose private equity ownership if they can.

Corrupt systems attract incompetent people. Well-governed systems attract competent people. There is a very positive self-selectivity among CEOs who choose private equity, for several reasons.

The first is the very powerful alignment of interest that runs like a steel chain right the way through the private equity ownership model.

And it starts with those CEOs and their fellow leadership executives in the underlying companies – and increasingly, the wider employees too.

To be the CEO of a private equity backed company is to be *all in*. There are no annual bonuses, and the salary is typically uncompetitive. Not just that, but you will be asked to *buy in to the buyout*, i.e. acquire a meaningful stake in the business. For most middle-market managers, this will involve taking out a sizeable loan or remortgaging their home. This is anti-fat-cattery in extreme form.

But there is a shiny flip side. They are also usually given 'sweet equity' – in other words, much more equity than the value of their buy-in. This is payment for future work. So, if all goes to plan, after five or so years, and the company is sold for a decent return, then add in the extra leverage of sweet equity, and a senior manager's return will be multiples larger. They might put in a few hundred thousand and get out tens of millions.

This is radical alignment of interest, and it works both ways. The upside is big but very uncertain (remember, these business executives aren't diversified across the whole fund portfolio. It's just this one company, and if it doesn't reach the performance hurdle, they are done.)

That's not their only downside risk.

If a company starts to underperform, most will have no hesitation at all to fire the CEO and find a replacement. That's why being a private equity backed CEO is a bit like riding a tiger. If your direction is aligned, you will benefit from a huge amount of power. But if you start to wobble, there will be no soft landing or rewards for failure.

In fact, if you want to talk about private equity leverage (and we will in Chapter 3), I would say this ability to fire and replace senior leadership is the biggest lever there is. Just imagine being able to fire a Fortune 500 CEO because you don't like the direction they are taking. Don't think of it as power. Think of it as radical, actionable accountability.

And this isn't theoretical. The CEO gets replaced in more than half of buyouts at some point during the ownership period, which is typically just three to five years.

The only thing more precarious than this is being a private equity backed CFO. That's because private equity managers tend to be micromanagers when it comes to things they really know about. And the things they really know about are numbers. The CFO is often the first person to be replaced.

This chain of brutal accountability forces everyone on that chain to pull in the same direction. The closer to the front you are – the CEOs, management teams and top employees – the bigger your effort, your risk and your potential reward. While those at the back of the chain – you, the investors who can diversify across multiple funds, managers and strategies – have the least effort, risk and reward. But the important point is this: broadly speaking, what is good for one should be good for all. There are no incentives to reduce short-term volatility in profits or protect plush jobs or perks. The steel chain of alignment pulls in one direction: towards maximising investor returns. This is key to the success of private markets.

Part II

Growth

In this section, we will look at different private markets investment strategies.

We will look at strategies that relate to the type of underlying asset: private equity, which is a way of owning profitable companies; there are strategies that play into the gaps and the corners of the private markets funds themselves – strategies like secondaries investment, co-investment and continuation funds. Next there is venture capital, which invests in start-ups; And finally, there is private credit – a strategy where you become the banker.

When you come to select a fund to invest in, you might choose a specific strategy (for instance by investing in a single-manager fund) or a fund that is diversified across several strategies and fund managers (funds-of-funds). Whichever is the case, you will want an understanding of the return drivers of each strategy, so you can make an informed decision about where you want to be, and why.

3

Big Beautiful Buyouts

'Give me a lever long enough and a fulcrum on which to place it, and I shall move the world'.

– **Archimedes**

We've said that LBOs are a lot like buying a house – let's quickly remind ourselves of the simple arithmetic of home mortgages. If you buy a house for $100k and sell it for $150k, you've made a 50% return. But if you use a 90% of debt (only $10k equity), you turn your $10k into $60k. That's a 6x return on equity - or a **500% profit** (minus interest repayments).

One early example is the 1982 buyout of Gibson Greeting Cards from a conglomerate called RCA by a buyout shop called Wesray. A young Lehman banker advising RCA, Stephen Schwarzman, told his client they were selling the business too cheap. (Schwarzman would later become the billionaire co-founder of KKR's main rival, the private markets giant Blackstone.) But the deal went ahead, and the buyout firm paid $80m for the company, using just $1m of equity. Sixteen months later, the market had improved significantly, and they sold the company for $290m. The two founders of Wesray had put in $600,000 and got back $65 million apiece.[1] The company owned the rights to Garfield the Cat, and this seems appropriate – the buyout merchants, it seemed, had gotten all the cream having barely lifted a paw.

Such examples are mind-boggling and perhaps, emotive, but not really representative of the returns of those early buyouts in general, some of which were fairly lacklustre as the economy turned sour in the early 1980s.

Indeed, somewhat ironically, KKR's colossal $25bn acquisition of tobacco company RJR Nabisco, which became the signature of an entire industry, and which, 40 years later, still looks implausibly massive, is thought to have made a small loss.

These early buyouts were vulnerable to the state of the market precisely because they were so reliant on leverage for driving returns. This made a deep impression on future generations of buyout investors. In the book *King of Capital*, the authors David Carey and John E. Morris reveal that Stephen Schwarzman regularly used RJR Nabisco as a cautionary tale to his colleagues. In other words, the private equity managers themselves rapidly became wary of using too much leverage in their deals. It was not in their interests to own companies that were not resilient to economic cycles.

But those first impressions have never really left the popular consciousness: ever since, private equity returns have been viewed as making obscene returns from 'just' financial engineering. But if this were the case, most of the upside would have quickly become arbitraged away in any case, either as public companies optimised their balance sheets (it's often forgotten that many large, listed companies today have high debt loads of 80% or more), or the market became flooded with buyout spreadsheet jockeys and financial engineers. There is no patent on financial innovation, and zero-sum advantages tend to be very fleeting. And yet four decades later, private equity is going from strength to strength. Something else is happening. (In fact, many things.)

But first, let's give 'the devil' its due: leverage continues to be a feature of most private markets investment, and for good reason. Leverage really serves two functions: to contribute to returns, but also as 'acquisition finance', where it serves more like a physical lever – to lift up heavy things (in this case, big companies) and move them to where you want them.

★

LBOs had been used for several decades before KKR, but nobody had paid much attention. The first two leveraged buyouts both happened in 1955. One was used by the company's own management to take control of Orkin Exterminating Company, a pest control business. The other was the acquisition of the Waterman Steamship Corporation by shipping magnate Daniel K Ludwig.

In other words, the LBO had already been 'invented', but it had only been used to help managers become owners and for industrialists to consolidate their position. It's 'killer-app' had not yet been discovered: giving power back to the owners of capital; aligning interests so that everybody is focused on the investment horizon and then getting on with the business of business.

The advantages of the LBO model when pursued as part of a portfolio of investments within a fixed-life, closed-ended LP fund constitute a model of such elegance and logic that you don't have to be Donald Trump to describe it as beautiful. No single consciousness put all these pieces together — it was a result of trial and error over long periods of time, of very slow adaptation and then natural selection of strategies that just work. Nobody foresaw the full logic of private equity LBOs in advance — its magic is only clear in retrospect.

★

Of course, it's not magic. Anybody can do it. It's just a question of incentives and 'norms'. When you are unconstrained, free to pursue productivity and don't have to worry too much about what other people think, leverage starts to lose its emotional charge.

Take Michael Dell, who we met in Chapter 2. The bespectacled Silicon Valley billionaire is a most unlikely barbarian. But in the good times, rather than using his billions to blast himself into space or buy up third world countries and islands like his billionaire chums, he set up a massive private equity programme (and as part of this, he was an early investor in the funds of Silver Lake). This experience meant he understood that you can do things in private markets that you just can't pull off in the glare of the public.

As Dell told *Fortune* magazine in 2021, if you have tonnes of capital on your balance sheet, it's hard to make your equity more valuable. 'But if you flip the equation . . . and say "Hey let's have a tech company with lots of debt" . . . with predictable cashflows, it's a winning strategy'. In total, he piled $70 billion of debt onto his growing corporate empire and transformed his business in the process.

★

We've spoken about the direct effect of leverage in juicing equity returns. But there are other important effects of the debt.

The first is that leverage removes temptation. By gearing up the balance sheet, private equity firms force the managers of the company to focus on profitability and cash flow in order to pay down the debt. Even if nothing else changed in the business, there would be no more cash for fleets of private jets and plush headquarters. It would have to be a very lean operation, efficient and focused on its goal. When a business is optimised, this enhanced efficiency and productivity is subject to a leverage effect as it then grows. This behavioural consequence of the LBO acquisition technique has proved enduringly powerful in influencing the behaviour of management teams of private equity backed companies over decades.

Some might complain that such constraint and discipline are 'fake' and unnecessarily burden companies with debt. But constraint is always necessary for the attainment of focused goals. Whether it is self-imposed or otherwise is beside the point.

But, say the critics, what about when inflation is high and interest rates go up. Now there will be entirely avoidable debt pressure on the company, which could, as a result, fail.

Maybe.

But if you have bought the right company in the first place, and you have not over-leveraged the business (which requires judgement), the inflationary nature of fiat currencies will mean that the leverage can work in your favour even in this scenario, so long as you have acquired a company with pricing power (i.e. that is able to rise its own prices in line with or above inflation/currency debasement). And this near-term positive exposure to inflation appears to be stronger for private markets assets than public assets.[2]

In addition, with the fiat currency on the liability side of the ledger, inflation works to erode the debt burden in real terms, as the equity compounds. It's probably not a huge effect and it doesn't apply all the time, but I labour the point because it is the opposite effect to that which is typically assumed.

Leverage is held by each individual portfolio company, not at the fund level, so each debt package is tailored to the specific company's cash profile, and as frequent users of corporate lending markets, private equity firms have become very sophisticated borrowers. They negotiate optimal interest rates and borrower-friendly covenants for each company and will regularly re-negotiate lending facilities during the life of the investment.

Unless the exit route is a (re)-listing, or they suspect that the trading environment may rapidly deteriorate, private equity firms will typically be in no hurry to de-lever. Why would they be? On the contrary, as a portfolio company increases its earnings and cash-generation over time, the private equity owners will often raise even more debt during the life of the investment and use the borrowings to pay their investors a dividend. This is known as a 'dividend recap' and it means the investors in the private equity fund get an income-like payment while the fund retains its full equity stake. It's standard fare in private markets, but quite shocking from a public markets context. This is understandable. Public markets are built to house established companies with very predictable sources of income and this should be reflected in either a steady growth in the value of shares or regular dividend payments, or both. Under these conditions, a one-off dividend funded with debt would be a red flag. But private equity firms aren't buying quasi-monopolies, they are rehabilitating flabby businesses or acquiring high-potential enterprises operating in dynamic environments.

Yet another benefit of the use of leverage is its tax treatment. In many countries, there is tax relief on corporate interest repayments to ensure that companies suffering trading difficulties are not unduly burdened. By deliberately loading up on debt, private equity firms can structure things so that their portfolio companies' interest repayments constitute a large part of a company's gross profits, meaning they end up paying very little tax. For those who want the government to spend other people's money, this is a source of irritation. For everyone else, it's another tick in the 'load me up' column.

★

Just Stock Markets Plus Leverage?

A casual and seductive criticism of private equity is that it's just a leveraged bet on the equity market.

The fact that the average outperformance (before fees) of private equity tends to be two to three times that of public equities, and they are also 2-3x more levered, provides superficial neatness to this concept.

But the argument assumes that leverage is zero-sum in terms of risk and return. Such a clear trade-off *may* apply in so-called 'efficient markets' but it categorically does not apply to private markets, which are inefficient, opaque and (most importantly) where companies are closely held and controlled.

The fallacy of the 'leveraged bet' argument can be seen simply by looking at the performance of the more indebted public companies relative to their index. If anything, they tend to underperform their peers.

The same principle applies whether you are applying DIY leverage to an individual stock or an index of stocks – you aren't in control of the business or the market. You might have done OK in the US stock market over the past few decades but the Japanese economy is emerging only now from a 30-year recession. And how confident are you that the US will see another multi-decade bull run, let alone China or Europe?

But hey, maybe it *is* worth a try, given that you will be dodging the huge fees that private markets funds absorb. There are funds out there, available to individual investors, that do precisely this – they track a stock market index, leverage up by about a third, and hedge away volatility.[3] Such funds may mimic private markets to some degree, but they are paper-barbarians – their tools are not being applied to the unchartered private markets, so they are not engaging with the same diversified opportunity-set. This really is a zero-sum activity.

The inconvenient truth is that very few types of equity owners can exploit financial leverage without taking on an equal and opposite amount of risk. Private markets managers are the exception, because they have control, and their cockpit has all sorts of levers for protecting their interests. (Public markets investors have just one, but it's not a lever, it's a big red button and it is marked 'Sell').

*

It's not that concerns around the use of leverage are entirely without merit. Of course, leverage does impose a burden on a company and this *could* make it more vulnerable should its core business weaken. And yes, there are examples of this happening – where private equity firms have made gross miscalculations in their company selection, their timing and then their application of leverage. If this was happening systematically or with anything like regularity, it would be reflected in private equity returns, and its sources of funds would quickly dry up. Cherry-picking bad examples is only a legitimate argument when you are dealing with a formula. But such examples are no more representative of 'private equity' than a few examples of public company failures are representative of 'public equity'. Private equity is not a formula or an equation. It is an activity that requires judgement.

You could argue that it would be better for everyone if all companies had less leverage and investors just accepted lower returns. When public market investors complain about private markets' leverage, they are arguing to bring the whole corporate and investment sphere down to the lowest common denominator. It is not a kindness to limp in the presence of the lame. Some use the term 'financial engineering' to dismiss the effect of leverage as zero-sum. But financial levers are no more zero-sum than physical levers. It is merely a more productive dispersion of pressure.

I advise private markets managers never to apologise for the use of leverage.

Clearly then, while acquisition finance is used as a lever to acquire companies, and this has captured the broader imagination, in a modern private equity context, corporate debt is less like a lever and more like a Swiss army knife at the end of a crowbar. Its uses are many and varied and in private markets, they are all deployed for the benefit of investment returns, not merely for the officers and agents who are hired to represent investor interests.

★

Leverage has its place, and it certainly contributes to performance, but in modern private equity, leverage is not the *major* driver of returns.[4] Leverage and debt-structuring skills are just table-stakes for private equity firms. It is what gets them through the door. It is one of the things that allows them to pay public market shareholders significantly more than the price at which the 'efficient' stock market values the company, so they can take it private, or so they can give hefty payouts to family-owners who want out. But once they have paid the premium and own the assets, that's just the beginning.

4

All Deals, Great and Small

'Conquering the world on horseback is easy. It is dismounting and governing that is hard'.

– Genghis Khan

It's always the mega deals that make all the headlines and become the focus of the best-selling novels. But as an investor, you don't care about how big the fish is. You care about how big your returns are, and in private equity, big returns can often come from small funds doing small deals. You might say, in the private markets ocean, quality trumps quantity. Sometimes whale blubber has value, but sometimes the smart money is in caviar.

The smallest types of deals in private markets are seed capital, usually for highly scalable tech companies. This is the world of venture capital that we look at in Chapter 6. But just within private equity, there is also a huge range of deal size and types, from minority investments in established business, to management buyouts of small and medium-sized companies, through to the mega LBOs of big businesses.

In fact, the private equity mid-market tends to take the lion's share of the action, because real, engaged equity ownership is not a naturally scalable activity. It's a hands-on, bottom-up endeavour, and the value comes not from minimising losses but maximising gains – and the biggest gains tend to come from businesses that aren't huge already. That's why the mid-market is often seen as private equity's hinterland and, while it might not get the headlines, it very often gets the big wins for investors.

Deep Sea Fishing

The mid-market is less a place than an idea. It isn't bounded by any specific deal size-range (indeed, both small and large buyout managers often claim to be 'mid-market' investors). The idea of the mid-market is of a realm of economic activity that involves real businesses that are larger than the millions of independent traders and micro-companies, but smaller than the mainly listed monoliths and monopolies. And it is a vast, deep ocean of opportunity, full of hidden treasures.

Private equity firms can invest in companies that are owned by families or have been built by entrepreneurs who are now seeking an exit or perhaps a deep-pocketed partner.

They can invest in unloved divisions of large corporations with divisional management teams brimming with ideas that they are unable to execute because they can't get it past head office.

They can invest in state-owned assets that have the potential to be economically viable private enterprises.

They can back private companies to buy other private companies in the same area, and merge them, creating bigger companies.

They even acquire companies from other private equity funds, in so-called secondary buyouts.

In other words, the theoretical investable universe for private equity firms constitutes almost the entire productive sphere of the economy. The private markets are a vast, deep ocean of opportunity.

Compare this to the public markets, where stock-pickers select from an overfished pool of listed companies, always with half an eye to casting them back and hooking another. But it's the same fish, over and over. They are even tagged with ticker symbols – you know, for efficiency. The stock markets are not oceans of opportunity but fish tanks of liquidity.

Deep sea fishing in private markets is a more serious affair. You don't take a rod and a deckchair. You need an armada with longlines, bait, sonar and supplies to last for months. Because not only is the sea vast, it is wine dark. There are no public reports or historic share prices (unless it's a take-private), no analyst or media coverage. Some opportunities aren't even recognisable as individual companies, they are embedded divisions of bigger entities. At these depths, just identifying the edges of the target can be difficult.

And there is no simple mechanism for acquiring a stake or monitoring performance. All this has to be done the hard way. Slowly, diligently.

Private equity firms can cast a very wide net, but they are also very picky fishermen. Most of what passes through their funnel, they throw back. This is partly because they can afford to – there is a lot of opportunity out there, and their return requirements are high.

They are also buying these companies outright, not just taking a tiny share, so they can afford to devote a huge amount of time and resources trying to find exactly the right company. This selection process is a major part of a private equity firm's activities, and once they have identified a company they like and there is a willing vendor, they will undertake a belts-and-braces due diligence process the likes of which is alien to most other types of investor. Given the importance of the incumbent management team to most modern buyouts, the due diligence process can verge on the invasive. A typical mid-market private equity firm will screen several hundred deals a year, they'll spend time on a few dozen and a lot of time on a handful. They might do just a couple of deals. And that's fine. Private equity is not a volume game; it is a value game.

(There is an internet meme among those acolytes of Benjamin Graham, the father of value investing, who are still trying to apply his teaching to public markets. It's a photo of someone casting his famous book, *The Intelligent Investor*, into the trash. But value investing is alive and well – just not so much on the stock market.)

Recognising Potential, Creating Value

I asked Todd Abbrecht, the current co-CEO of Thomas H Lee Partners (now called THL Partners), which was established a year before KKR and may therefore be the first ever modern private equity firm, what the secret of private equity's success is. His answer: 'evolution'. Over 50 years, his firm – and others – have evolved and adapted to provide strong returns to investors, throughout credit cycles and economic crises. If buyouts were a one-trick pony, a balance sheet trick, they wouldn't have made it past the early 1980s.

The real value in private equity is being created in the fundamental business and operations of each company they acquire.

Competition to buy good companies is fierce. This is the so-called 'mergers & acquisitions' market. (Really, there is no such thing as a merger, one company always acquires another.) Private equity's competitor is often large companies looking to make acquisitions. In theory, such corporate acquirers have an advantage over private equity, because they will benefit from operational synergies. But in practice, there are all sorts of organisational, strategic and bureaucratic reasons why corporates often don't show up or show up with the right number. That's why the most consistent form of competition for private equity firms is other private equity firms.

Most companies (even small ones) are sold via carefully stage-managed auction processes, which proceed through various rounds of bidding, over several months. It's easy for any private equity firm to win these auctions by overpaying. Clearly, the trick is to find a reason for a business to be more valuable to your firm than to others. The finance industry tries to make valuation a science, but in essence, it is an art and in the eye of the beholder, because 'a fool sees not the same tree a wise man sees'.

Most private equity firms will want to back the management team's plan. Often, a good management team will know what needs to be done to unlock the potential, and the simple fact of having a single, attentive, controlling shareholder means they can act quickly and without bureaucratic restraint to unleash that value.

But if that's all there was to it, the only way to pay more than any other private equity firm would be to reduce your returns. That's the calculus of the Efficient Markets Hypothesis, on which mainstream investment thinking is based. It applies to markets where all participants have equal knowledge, resources, connections, creativity and where this is all baked into the price. This is not at all a description of private markets, which are not remotely efficient. And that's a good thing, because value lurks where inefficiency reigns. It's what happens after the deal is signed that matters most. Private equity isn't a way of buying companies (that's just an 'LBO'). It's a way of owning them to ensure they reach their full potential. The industry refers to this process as 'value creation' but you might just think of it as getting on with business without unnecessary distractions.

From the moment the ink is dry on the deal (and actually, even before), a private equity deal is a race to realise that potential. The first few months are often treated as a sprint to get the company on the right footing: removing inefficiencies, getting in the right people and organisational structure that will support ongoing efforts to grow the business.

Most private equity firms will have a dedicated team of operational specialists who will act something like external advisers to the company, with specific subject-matter expertise that is relevant to most businesses that they acquire.

For instance, they may have experts in pricing, in talent acquisition (recruitment), in balance sheet optimisation (improving capital efficiency and unlocking trapped cash), in outsourcing, digitisation and AI. As private equity firms compete with each other, so their sophistication in these areas has grown. Early in my career, one private equity manager explained to me that the secret behind his success when his firm acquired the Mumm Champagne brand in 1999 was that they raised the prices, and as a luxury (or 'Giffen') good, its perceived value also increased. And that's how they did it. I mean, *why didn't I think of that?* These days, pricing is a science more than an art form, with private equity firms deploying big data and cutting-edge analytical tools to optimise pricing.

In the old days, there was also more emphasis on cutting costs – after all, most businesses are somewhat inefficient, and making them more efficient is an easy win. But in today's mature and competitive M&A marketplace, if efficiency via cost-cutting is your priority, you will fail to deliver the returns necessary to raise future funds. That's why private equity firms see an efficient operating model less through the lens of cost and more as to whether it will provide an effective foundation for growth.

Some private equity firms will still fall for the temptation to get quick wins by myopically cutting costs. But these days, I suspect a more common error is to underestimate the cost of new investment projects. One large buyout firm told me that when they bought a brand name consumer business, their initial value-creation plan under-budgeted the cost of building a new CRM by tens of millions. (Thankfully, everything else went so well, it didn't matter much in the end.)

Everyone used to talk about the first 100 days, which was when most disruptive actions would take place, and then the company would have a few years to bed down and develop more or less organically. Today, active engagement and optimisation are more or less ongoing. This is particularly the case with private equity backed companies that pursue a 'buy and build' strategy.

Buying, Building, Rolling

The buy-and-build model brings us full circle from the first wave of conglomerate-smashing barbarians. You buy a company (usually the market leader or second best) in an industry that is fragmented and where a dominant player would derive a size advantage or even monopolistic benefits. Then you back that company as a 'platform' to buy (or 'roll-up') its competitors. Each time, you benefit from cost synergies, cross-selling synergies, brand awareness, geographic expansion, some diversification and eventually more pricing power.

Not just that, but bigger companies (all else being equal) fetch a higher price (i.e. a higher valuation relative to their earnings) than smaller companies. (This applies to any company that grows in size, not just buy-and-builds – but these tend to grow their top-line faster, because they are buying revenue.) This phenomenon is called 'multiple arbitrage' but that is a weak description, because it's not arbitrage, it's another kind of leverage. It is *valuation leverage*.

It's all very simple in theory – harder in practice. You have to integrate different systems, processes, brands and (hardest of all) cultures. I know some companies that have done dozens of these add-on acquisitions in the space of a few years. Others have done very well by doing just one larger acquisition that proves transformative in their market. To me, it sounds like a lot of work, and I don't think your average company manager would consider it worth the hassle. But now imagine you've bought into a buyout, alongside a deep-pocketed private equity firm, and they've given you sweet equity (labour leverage). Now you add on valuation leverage. And yes, old-fashioned financial leverage.

There is a mirror-image strategy to these buy-and-build or 'roll-up' strategies, and that's a roll-*out* strategy. Are you keeping up? The idea is to rapidly expand a consumer business, such as a restaurant chain, clothing shop or branded coffee shop, by coming up with a formula that you repeat in new locations. In this case, you aren't buying other companies, you are finding the right real estate and then colonising it. Any type of investor can do this in theory, but private equity has really taken it to heart. It requires systematisation, deep pockets, an appetite for risk, discipline around costs, a focus on operational efficiency, strong monitoring and governance. But when it works, it really works. You will be familiar with examples of this, depending on where you live: Pizza Express was an early example in the UK. There's now a Yo! Sushi in every retail complex and a Pret a Manger on every other street corner, thanks to private equity. In the US, there are Dunkin' Doughnuts, Burger King and TGI Fridays. In Japan, there is Sushiro, while in China, Luckin Coffee opened 4,500 stores in just three years under private equity ownership!

Private Sequels

As the private equity landscape has matured, when it's time to realise an investment in a company, very often the keenest buyers can be other private equity firms. What better proof of the fundamental value being created by the model than other, independent, private equity firms wanting to take on the assets. Oddly enough, the establishment media often take it to mean they are merely 'passing the parcel' among themselves. It is a reading that follows a fundamental misunderstanding of the fiercely competitive and independent structure of the industry and the funds.

Such deals are often referred to as secondary buyouts, but this is confusing and misleading, partly because such companies can go through several phases of private equity ownership and partly because 'secondaries' means something else, which we will come on to. They are more like sequels.

There is a more interesting critique of this intra private equity dealmaking: it's very inefficient. If there is still potential to be realised, why would a private equity firm sell? The simple answer is that they must in order to achieve a realisation that returns capital to investors and allows them to wind down the fund. But that just speaks to the inefficiency of the fund structure.

Here is the more fundamental reason for such sequential deals. In complex situations, optimisation can be a trap. The value creation process isn't systematic – it isn't a technique or playbook that can just be followed. It is primarily a function of incentives and human effort and endeavour. The cadence of a private equity investment, which runs for three to five years, is something like a marathon run at a sprint. By the end of that period, there needs to be a reset – of incentives and compensations, as well as of minds, spirits and creativity. Such psychological factors are central to success.

A hard realisation also reduces the incidence of fraud, since the books are opened and examined so intently upon sale. Fraud in private equity firms and their underlying assets is rare indeed.

When a new private equity firm takes over a sequential target, it will come with fresh perspectives and new energy. It will also often have more financial firepower (since it is likely to be a bigger fund), different connections, perhaps a more international scope and so on. Private equity isn't a game that goes on forever without reference to other ownership structures, but it can go on for a very long time. In fact, it has the fundamental hallmarks of a moral enterprise: it is an iterative game that gets better the longer it is played.

The Same. But Different

I've spent a lot of time with various private equity firms, helping them to articulate their unique approach to the market (primarily so they can raise fresh funds – it's not easy raising blind pools of capital every few years.) It is always an interesting sales challenge because, on the face of it, private equity firms can often end up saying the exact same thing (more or less the value creation tools I've just outlined). It can sometimes feel like observing the different techniques among a room full of painters – but from the front of the class, so you are blind to their work. From that perspective, they are all identical, since they all use a paintbrush, some canvas. . . water is very important too. What this misses is the element that is not quantifiable. To see that, you must go to the back of the class – and see that each painter/private equity firm has a completely unique style and approach that cannot be revealed mechanistically. It is a human and cultural quality and it *can* be conveyed, but not in a quantitative, wholly objective manner. Therefore, selecting a good fund manager as an LP investor involves soft skills that are not always fully appreciated.

Niches, Playbooks and Arbitrage

The holy grail for any private equity firm isn't just to find a strategy that works – it's to find one that is repeatable. If you can crack the code of a sector or a theme, that is a winning lottery ticket. It has the effect of making your blind-pool fundraising a much safer prospect. (Of course, nothing lasts forever.)

For example, not so long ago, 'Hg' was a fairly generalist buyout house. But it hit upon a replicable approach to creating value, particularly in software and tech-enabled services. It uses a highly systematic approach to sourcing and scaling recurring-revenue software companies with high margins, low churn and then rolling up fragmented sectors. Today, if Hg were a software company, it would be the second largest in Europe.

Similarly, when private equity firms identify sectors and themes with the right characteristics, they will all pile in. But there is a downside to this somewhat herd mentality: private equity firms can sometimes be slow at adopting genuinely new technologies. For instance, with some exceptions, they have been slow at pushing the adoption of AI in their own processes and that of their companies.

Bureaucracy Arbitrage

There is one way they make money that nobody ever acknowledges out loud, and for me, it gets to the essence of private equity's nature. I think of it as 'bureaucracy arbitrage'.

About 20 years ago, new regulations for insurers in Europe meant they wanted to get out of the 'enhanced annuities' business – it had become too expensive for them, from a cost of capital perspective. This, combined with secular trends such as an ageing demographic and pension changes, meant there was a huge market opportunity to soak up, but almost everybody with the requisite knowledge and skills was 'in the insurance industry' and not in a position to exploit it. Cinven, a UK buyout house, spotted it. They backed a pure play business in the UK called Partnership Assurance, before floating it on the stock exchange. They then did something similar with a company called Guardian, before going to Germany and doing it all again with a company called Viridium.

These are situations that private equity firms can exploit simply because of the freedom afforded by their committed source of capital and the fact that they are unencumbered by legacy baggage.

And now the power of simple, aligned models of governance comes into view. The fatalism of the 'Efficient Markets Hypothesis' that dominates so much public markets thinking – that everything is baked in, you can't win, you can't draw and you can't quit the game – it just isn't true, at least for private markets. You can enhance value without a commensurate increase in risk, so long as you operate with the right guiding principles. That's what private equity comes down to – and why we spent so long looking at the funding model. Private equity is not a way to buy companies or do anything in particular to them – whether it's flip, strip, leverage, roll-up, roll-out, buy-out, build-up or grow. It is just a system of company governance, ownership and oversight, based on simple principles of good and fair conduct.

For insight into funds that provide exposure to private equity deals (from small to mega) and that are available for investment by qualifying individual investors, scan this QR code.

5

Real Deals and Guerrillas

'The difficulty in tactical manoeuvring consists in turning the devious into the direct, and misfortune into gain'.

– Sun Tzu

No one likes middlemen – but cutting them out can be highly counterproductive when the stakes are high, the landscape complex and trust and relationships drive the market. Their value often lies not in the product itself, but in access, timing and expertise.

In private markets, there are several intermediaries notably funds of funds managers, who handle the onerous task of making commitments to 'primary' funds. But in addition to this somewhat administrative function, their real value is in tactically exploiting market inefficiencies. They are less like barbarians and more like guerrilla fighters. To understand their value better, we should look closer at the role of the investor in classic fixed-life, closed-end funds – the limited partner or LP.

So far, we have described these LPs as essentially passive – the sedentary partner. But in modern private markets, this does them a disservice. There is much skill and effort involved in managing a large portfolio of private markets funds. More than that, there is much value to be harvested from tactical manoeuvres in the fund world.

But first, let's look at the operational requirements.

Even knowing who is out there, raising funds in the market, is not always easy. You need to be connected. There are no comprehensive listings and even if you found one you wanted to invest in, you can't just transact and buy in. Each fund commitment is a privately negotiated contract. In terms of hassle, it's a lot more like buying a house than a stock (although it is becoming much easier for individuals, as we will see in Chapter 8).

Then there are the minimum commitment levels of classic funds, which are usually $5m and sometimes more. And to have a well-managed and diversified programme, you are going to be spending $5m quite frequently. For instance, not only will you want a mix of equity and credit funds, but just within equity, there are buyouts, growth capital and venture capital. Within each, there are sector-specialist funds, like healthcare venture capital or financial services buyouts. Then there are those who focus only on the United States, or maybe Northern Europe. Then there are infrastructure funds, real estate, natural resources and all the different layers of credit – mezzanine, distressed, direct, investment-grade. Even a relatively concentrated programme will be quite the capital commitment. But that's not all.

The temporary nature of such funds (that anti-fragile feature that is so inconvenient and essential) means that private markets have a third dimension of complexity to manage: time. An investment programme must commit to funds consistently, over time, or else be exposed to specific 'vintages' – or moments in the economic cycle. So this isn't a one-off capital commitment; it is ongoing.

An even bigger headache than this is managing cashflows. . . . The great thing about private market funds is that they return hard cash. But be careful what you wish for. If you keep getting your money back, you have to keep investing it. That means you must perpetually find new funds to invest in. As an LP, you can't just invest and hold forever.

There is a final drag that LPs must deal with, and that is cash itself. You'll remember that first you commit, then the GP finds things to invest in. As a result, there can be a delay of several years between making a commitment and being fully invested. Meanwhile, the commitment has to be ready and waiting, usually in cash, and remember, cash is trash. To solve this, LPs forecast the returns they expect to get from other funds, and then effectively 'over-commit' their programme. Only by doing this can they ensure they will be fully invested at any one time.

So that's the stuff that all LP programmes must contend with – it is a hamster-wheel of technical challenges, none of which are beyond the wit of man, but they also constitute a real operational burden.

These fund constraints can also be a pain for GP fund managers. While I have opined at length about the wonders of the classical LP fund commitment, during periods of extended downturns, things can get strained. For instance, after the Covid lockdowns, market euphoria saw private markets funds raise and spend several years' worth of capital in a short time frame. Then markets fell – a bad time to realise investments. And ever since, up to the time of writing in mid-2025, there has just been (to coin a phrase) 'one damn thing after another', keeping market prices depressed. So GPs still don't want to sell, even though their funds are getting rather old, and unless their LPs can get some money back from the current crop of investments, they won't be able to raise any new funds. Meanwhile, investors such as pension funds, are getting impatient, prompting a nerdy industry meme, 'IRR < DPI', which basically translates to, *thanks for the uplift on paper, now just give me the damn money!*

So occasionally, the private markets get an acute indigestion, and like indigestion, it's a pain but it won't kill you. But this is precisely the type of opportunity that the guerrilla investor can exploit.

Recent years have seen a flood of strategies that allow GPs to 'show some gains' without really selling companies. For instance, they have been raising finance against the value of their unrealised portfolio (such as 'NAV financing', 'equity bridge financing' and 'sub-lines'). For asset managers who understand the markets, know the managers and their specific positions and motivations, financing such deals can be lucrative.

Another increasingly popular guerrilla tactic is to invest in a continuation fund. The situation is usually where a GP has a crown jewel, its favourite investment, and it believes there is plenty more value in it that will take more time than they have – remember they need to sell and return all capital eventually. So instead, they find an LP to create a new single-asset fund, and they both co-invest and re-invest in the asset.

You may even be a part of the solution to the gummed-up exit markets, given that so many managers are setting up new unlisted evergreen vehicles – as the cash flows in, these need to buy *something* (see Chapter 9).

The performance potential of primary deals like buyouts or venture capital is, in some sense, obvious. But you could argue that the real outperformance, the real edge, comes from identifying tactical opportunities lurking in the dark, illiquid corners of the markets and exploiting them ruthlessly. If that sounds good to you, find yourself a guerrilla-style asset manager who can demonstrate a tactical approach to private market fund opportunities beyond 'primary' commitments.

Secondaries: Taking Candy from Big Babies

For instance, at any one time, there are many forlorn LPs who no longer want to commit. They've changed their mind and need to exit the market before their investments have ripened. Take Harvard, for example. Its university endowment has done very well indeed from its private markets exposure since the 1980s, to the extent that it has been called a multi-billion-dollar hedge fund with a business school attached. But in 2016, it decided to restructure its programme. Among the concerns, apparently the programme was too expensive to run, because their internal private equity specialists had good salaries. The private markets portion of their portfolio also did not apparently fall hard enough during the global financial crisis, which made the rest of their portfolio look bad, and for some institutions, a lack of conformity to either the upside or the downside is not welcomed.

Then the final straw: in the face of Trump II funding cuts, Harvard's endowment decided it needed to sell off (a small) part of its private equity portfolio. But when it came to market, it found that it could only sell its commitments at a discount to face value. Its $53bn endowment, it turned out, was actually worth more like $40bn, claimed Harvard alumnus, billionaire investor Bill Ackman. He argued that, as a result, the whole market should be downgraded.

These are just the kind of opportunities that your guerrilla investor lives for. By acquiring such 'secondary' LP interests at a discount to their face value, such intermediaries acquire all the upside of private markets assets, plus the bonus of buying them below fair value, and so juice the returns for their investors.

Ironically enough, a major proportion of frontline private markets barbarians are Harvard alumni. You would have thought one of them could have sent a memo. They could have called it 'How do you like your chicken cooked?'

> *If you buy a chicken for $10, then take it out the oven half-cooked and eat it, don't go around saying chickens are risky and barely worth $7.*

The idea that only individuals can be foolish and improvident, while institutions are sensible and long-term oriented, is the starting point of much financial regulation. But institutions are capable of just as much myopia and impulsivity, compounded by ideological motives that are unconstrained by economic self-interest – since they aren't investing their own money. But the silver lining is that individual investors can now be on the right side of that trade.

In addition, with secondaries, because you are buying funds that are up and running, they are not 'blind pools' but funds with assets in, so you know what you are buying. This also means there is no delay or 'J-curve' in putting your money to work.

The next big wave of secondaries opportunities might not be in private equity at all. Private credit is growing fast, and it is much more scalable than equity. But private credit secondaries are growing even faster. There can be many motivations for selling secondaries, but at the time of writing, much activity was being led by GPs themselves, who are bundling up anything from a few dozen to hundreds of credits and selling them to continuation vehicles. All this type of novel structuring doesn't just keep lawyers busy (although it does.) It also presents a big opportunity for guerrilla-style asset managers, who take a multi-strategy, multi-asset, multi-manager, bird's-eye view of the market and swoop on structural inefficiencies (of which there are so very many in private markets) in order to boost returns.

Co-invest and Other Flanking Manoeuvres

Asset managers can also find strategic angles by working alongside GPs that they have good relationships with. For instance, in addition to providing funds as an LP, they can co-invest in specific deals alongside the GP - outside of the fund. For the GP, it increases their firepower - say if they want to buy a bigger company than usual. They wouldn't want to use a competitor so a solution is to allow an LP to add equity on the same terms as the GP (in fact better, because the deal is pre-screened) and to do so without paying the management fee or the carried interest. (But it is also more concentration risk, so the guerrilla asset manager needs the capability to not only assess frontline barbarians, but underlying investments too.)

This is also a growing market for 'GP stakes': not investing in LP funds but buying a share in the manager itself. (It can be something of a sell-out on the part of the founders, since they are giving away part of the carried interest pool in perpetuity. On the other hand, they are often bringing on board a minority shareholder who can add firepower to future fundraises.) There are even specialist funds that only invest in GP stakes. I've even heard of one who takes stakes in GP stakes managers. Very meta.

Top asset managers will also be on the lookout for new talent – so-called emerging managers: people spinning out to form new funds and pursue new strategies. Getting in early can mean preferential funding terms (i.e. lower fees or even participation) and early access to deal flow and co-investment opportunities, as well as being well positioned should the manager continue to grow.

The more skilful and confident the manager is at operating within private markets, the more value-creating opportunities they will find. Much of this activity you will not read about. It does not make the newspapers and even the data providers don't pick it up. It is the shadow private market, and it can be a source of significant value.

For insight into funds that provide exposure to real deals – from specialist funds such as secondaries and co-invest through to those providing opportunistic and diversified private markets exposure that are available for investment by qualifying individual investors – scan this QR code.

6

Risk It for the Biscuit

'If you're afraid, don't do it. If you're doing it, don't be afraid'.
— **Genghis Khan**

Encouraging children to own, handle and use sharp knives is generally considered something of a no-no — except in Scandinavia, where many children, even very young ones, are often 'carrying'. And travellers note that extremely young children tend to travel alone in countries such as Japan and Switzerland. In the Anglosphere, most kindergarteners would find themselves in police custody before making it to the bus stop. *'But where's your Mummy?!'*

You might say it's just cultural, but it's more than this because risk-taking behaviours only lose their taboo when they are accompanied by the skills and competence required to mitigate that risk.

That is the case with start-up company investment in the form of venture capital.

Investing in new companies is extremely risky. Most start-ups fail in their first few years and, of those that survive to have people and offices, few of them make it beyond 10 employees, because companies experience a founder-bottleneck and can't professionalise.

If you can make it to 50 or so employees, you are usually considered an SME (small or medium-sized enterprise), and the risk of failure declines significantly, but vanishingly few of these will make it big (and from a naïve investment perspective, nowhere near enough will get big to offset all the other failures).

Company size follows a power law, whereby a tiny number of companies become giants of their age and their industry (think Google or IBM or Ford), and then there is a very, very 'long tail' of also-rans. Companies with fewer than 20 employees constitute about 90% of most developed economies. In the United States, companies with more than 500 employees constitute less than 0.5% of the economy, and yet they employ about half of all workers.

Given that investing in start-up companies is about betting on which new ideas are going to be the big companies of tomorrow, all things being equal, the odds are beyond terrible. But all things are not equal.

Venture capital fund investment constitutes a sophisticated and layered process, with risk being mitigated or dissipated at each level, while successes are followed, nourished and scaled. Let's look at how it works.

In the old days, the process of raising capital was somewhat linear. When a first-time entrepreneur needed capital for a new venture, their first port of call was 'friends, family and fools'. If they didn't lose all their money, they might then be able to attract a wealthy individual to invest some equity. These people are 'business angels'. This is still very risky, and one suspects their motivation is similar to that of the theatre backers, from which they get their name: the emotional thrill and kudos of the odd success, which compensates for overall investment mediocrity. If the company was still growing quickly and had a really good story to tell about their growth potential, they might then attract their first 'institutional' capital, from a venture capital firm.

Venture capital firms were (and to a large degree, still are) extremely picky. Their refusal rate is extremely high, probably above 99%. And this is the chief skill of the venture capital executive: selection. This is not a due diligence exercise. When you are investing in growth potential, there is nothing 'due' to be 'diligent' about. Rather it is about pattern recognition, proprietary knowledge and insight, technical expertise and crucially, intuition.

Again, in the old days, the venture capital calculus was that they would invest in 10–20 companies per fund. About half would fail, a few would do OK and one or two would be so successful that they would 'bring home' the whole fund.

An early example of this was Benchmark Capital's first fund of $85m. It invested in a dozen or more companies and it would have been a very mediocre affair – were it not for one thing. They bought a 22% stake in eBay for $7m. That one call made it a 100x fund, utterly eclipsing all the other failures and also-rans in their portfolio, and indeed all other venture capital funds of that vintage.

You will notice from this that not only is company survival a power law, but so are venture capital returns. Peter Thiel, the founder of PayPal, famously pointed this out in his book *Zero to One*, and this was a welcome observation for venture capitalists (VCs) because it meant that their seemingly haphazard way of making returns actually had some statistical basis.

★

Biologists split species reproduction and survival strategies into two types: r-type selectors and k-type selectors.[1]

K-type selectors are suited to stable and predictable environments. They have a small number of offspring, since the risk of loss is low, and spend a large amount of resources nurturing them. Modern humans are k-type selectors, as are private equity investors.

R-type selectors are suited to unstable and unpredictable environments, where there is a high risk of loss. They will have a very high birth rate, a very high infant mortality rate, and they will spend little to no time on parental care. Mosquitoes and sharks fall into this category. It's a 'grow fast or die' creed.

VCs effectively realised that being too k-type in their behaviour, like their private equity cousins, did not optimise the power law nature of their model. Therefore, over the past two decades, most big venture capital firms have pivoted to be more r-type in their initial investment behaviour: seeding dozens or scores of start-ups and offering minimal support. These micro investments are almost like call options, a right to invest more if a company does well. Then they will watch. The weak and the average and even the fairly good, these will be allowed to starve. The ones that show real promise will get all the attention. In other words, they will start as r-type and then switch to k-type selectors. K-type parents who have favourites.

They are still super selective, but the big venture firms with large capital resources can afford to be initially promiscuous, spreading small amounts of cash among more promising ideas. It's a recognition, of course, that early-stage company investment is a radically uncertain activity. There is no formula or monopoly on getting it right. They have therefore adopted (consciously or not, I don't know) natural selection-type behaviours to help minimise risk without materially compromising returns.

Of course, evolution doesn't happen gradually; it requires step-changes. Venture capital's mutation came with the creation of a Californian start-up accelerator in 2005. Before Y Combinator, incubators were a forgettable part of the venture ecosystem, akin to a perk you get from taking on shared office space. But Y Combinator was different. Up to that point, most start-ups raised money by pitching directly to angels and VCs. Y Combinator formalised short, structured programmes to prepare founders that it pre-selected, and then allowed them to pitch to hundreds of VCs at once, in two batches a year that are akin to an American football style 'draft'.

The YC funding is very formulaic, with fixed equity stakes for fixed investments. They created a simple formula to ensure early investors could follow their money without getting diluted.

The model became rapidly popular and was scaled under the leadership of Sam Altman. It has been responsible for launching many well-known venture successes, including Airbnb, Stripe, Dropbox, Reddit, Coinbase and OpenAI. In so doing, it transformed venture capital in a number of ways.

Firstly, it radically increased competition for funding at a very early stage, which had previously been the hardest money to raise. Its standardised investment terms stripped away a lot of the transactional complexity that had previously characterised the market. And it radically reduced due diligence cycles, which had previously been closer to private equity's very legalistic approach. It took away this crutch from VCs and forced them to acknowledge what had always been the case: that when faced with radical uncertainty, judgement, pattern recognition and split-second intuition are worth ten thousand billable hours.

That Feeling of Weightlessness

The need for huge wins obviously influences not just the specific companies that venture capital focuses on, but the company types and the sectors. Obviously, the business model itself has to be scalable. In previous decades and centuries, they might have backed chemical companies or automakers or railroads. Today, it's obviously all tech, and mainly software, applications, digital services and online businesses – companies that operate in what one venture capitalist, Patrick Sheehan of the Environmental Technologies Fund, has called the 'intelligence layer' of modern economies. Those that have a close-to-zero incremental cost of sale. Apple, for example, can deliver its latest software package to a billion people, in one night, effectively for free.

In Patrick's estimation, successful venture firms focus on companies that are as weightless as possible. 'Innovations based on electrons have steeper and more predictable learning curves than those based on molecules', he says. It's why we have insanely smart AI but still no flying cars. We might still get flying cars, but it's unlikely venture capital will be the main backer, because it would constitute too great a financial investment and a financial risk for them. (That's why it often takes bootstrapped entrepreneurs to build those extremely rare physical tech companies, like Dyson with his re-imagined vacuum cleaners and Musk with his re-imagined space/travel.)

Biotech venture funds might take issue with this characterisation of molecular innovation-malfunction, and if you have a medical background or believe that such innovations would sit well in your portfolio, there will be plenty of venture fund opportunities for you to choose from in this domain. But beware that such areas of innovation are particularly challenging, typically requiring more investment and lower capital efficiency compared to, say, software, and very long timelines. You can burn through $100m on biotech research in no time flat.

I personally think the anti-molecule bias is borne out by the evidence. There have been no significant innovations in the treatment of major rich world diseases such as cancer, dementia or Alzheimer's research for decades. By contrast, there have been huge advances in knowledge about the causes of such diseases (lifestyle choices, for example). But the commercial opportunities around such prevention (wearable tech, for instance) are limited – and in any case bring us back to atoms and bits.

★

In a risky world – one characterised by perpetual technological disruption – you can try to avoid risk, let's say by hiding in sectors that seem immune to disruption and innovation. Or you can have a stake in the fortunes of those frontline venturers who have made it their business to understand that risk, to manage it and to profit from everyone else's disruption.

There are many ways venture capital firms mitigate risk and enhance their returns. The most uninspiring ways are around contracting – such as making sure they have powerful, if not controlling, rights in a company, even if they aren't taking a majority stake.

But sometimes, the deck is just more favourably stacked than it appears from the outside. When I was a rookie reporter in 2002, I covered an early-stage venture capital investment in a French start-up that was delivering DVDs by mail order. Trust me, it was cutting edge. I asked the VC why they thought it was a good investment and I was deflated to learn that they were just copying the business model of a company that had, earlier that month, listed on Nasdaq. It was called Netflix. The French company was subsequently acquired by the UK's Lovefilm, which was then acquired by Amazon. It's not an investment strategy that was going to save the human race, but you can't have it both ways.

Venture Capital Fund Returns

Even after all this, the outcome of an individual venture capital fund is still a risky prospect. About a third of them actually lose money (not all of it, they just don't make a return). About half of them break even or make a modest gain. But the top 10% funds bring home all the bacon because, you guessed it, venture capital at the level of fund investment is also a power law. And that's what makes venture capital fund investment a much more interesting investment prospect than it first appears.

Institutional investors in any part of the private markets will never be invested in one fund, managed by one manager, in one strategy, in one vintage, in one geography, in one sector. It is this diversification within a market dominated by power laws that introduces the layer of risk-mitigation that takes us from radically uncertain outcomes to statistical probabilities of success. One big win, one 100x-er, and you have a return that cannot be replicated anywhere else in the markets without taking on some form of zero-sum financial risk.

In addition, there appears to be a significantly greater performance persistence in venture capital than in any other part of the private (or public) markets. In other words, a manager with a fund in the top quartile is likely to have its next fund at least in the top half. This could be because of the advantages of scale and the ability to follow their money. It could also be that the large venture capital firms carry an aura that can be enough to help young companies attract big customers and increase their chances of survival.

The variety of venture capital strategies are truly vast – from early-stage and seed specialists through to the full-spectrum Silicon Valley firms; there are even buyout groups with venture arms. There are venture firms specialising in software, biotech, climate tech, deep tech, AI, space and satellites, fintech, crypto, cannabis, as well as many generalists focused on specific geographies. There are VCs focused on solving specific problems, such as environmental degradation or those of an ageing population, and hyper-niche players, such as video game investors.

Making an Impact

With venture capital, and this is true of most private markets to a degree, you are not dealing with an impersonal, efficient-market-type calculation. Everything is contextualised and that means it is about people and real-world impact.

Impact has become a loaded term, but it shouldn't be. It's just meant to mean 'doing good in the world'. It is unfortunate that many people feel the need to separate this concept from 'investing for returns', because if you are engaged in genuine investment aimed at productive enterprise, rather than speculation, then there should be very little difference. More to the point for venture capital, investing for an intentional, measurable positive social or environmental return is challenging because the activity of backing start-ups, itself, is so inherently uncertain. Seeking to extract 'impact' or identify the intention in advance is typically not the most meaningful of exercises. It's always done with the best of intentions, but there are costs: this separation of impact and returns introduces all types of complexities into an investment context that is quite complex enough. For one, it encourages a form of corporate virtue signalling that is typically hyperbole if not pure fantasy. (This is even more true in private equity than venture.) And it introduces confusion around the commitment of a fund to produce returns versus other lesser goals that cannot be defined with objective measures (like sustainable profits) and this threatens to break the chain of alignment and fiduciary duty in fund management.

This fuzzy approach can be compounded by poor regulation. For instance, the EU's Sustainability Finance Disclosure Regime ranks funds according to their environmental credentials. They are de-rated if they invest in high-polluting companies – the perfect disincentive to do what private markets do best: take inefficient companies and improve them.

It is obviously the case that some strategies will be more beneficial to the human condition than others. But as an investor, the only way to assess this, rather than to trust in labels ('impact' and 'ESG', 'sustainable investment'), is to actually look at what the fund manager is doing. It will quickly become apparent whether your ethical considerations are in alignment.

Venture Statism

To state the obvious, the link between impact and returns is strongest when it is guided by potential demand. This is nicely summed up in Y Combinator's strapline: 'Make something people want'. But there can be a disconnect when your main customer, investor or influencer is the state.

From its name, you might think venture capital is the ultimate in unconstrained, free-market enterprising. Oddly enough, almost the opposite is the case. Government interference in venture capital is almost endemic, almost everywhere in the world. This can be for good and ill.

In the United States, the state support has been vast but relatively subtle and indirect. The US military-industrial complex has been a major customer to Silicon Valley, and the early VCs were ex-soldiers. Most of the major technologies that built the modern world were formed in this crucible. The direct forerunner to the internet, Arpanet, was a US Department of Defense programme to improve communication between defence researchers. GPS was funded and built by the Department of Defense, and US state military expenditure also drove the major advances in mRNA, encryption, digital imaging and sensors, drones and voice recognition.

Even semiconductors and microprocessors – the very backbone of the information age – were funded by the US Department of Defense. (This, together with the DoD's development of the modern shipping container in the 1950s, gives it claim to be the father of the modern technologised global economy. It's a whole secret history.)

As well as funding the deep tech, the US state is also a very helpful early customer for young tech companies. This is partly enshrined in federal law, given that the Small Business Act requires more than a fifth of the federal budget to be spent with small and medium-sized businesses. Even large contractors must commit to a flow-down arrangement to use a proportion of smaller subcontractors.

Military spending has been a major supply-side stimulant and competitive advantage to the US venture capital industry. You could argue that the real backer of US venture capital over the past 50 years has been US Treasury bills.

Unlike in private equity, there tends to be an observable outperformance of US venture capital versus the rest of the world. There are endless debates as to why this is the case, and it usually revolves around 'entrepreneurial spirit', 'red tape' and lack of growth-oriented public markets – all of which are undoubtedly true. It's much less observed, but having a money-printing war machine as your first customer might also be a contributing factor.

Europe, on the other hand, is almost a mirror image of this in every dimension. On a continent that has always had an ambivalent relationship with capitalism, policymakers view venture capital as its (just-about) acceptable face. But they don't like venture capital *itself* but how it could deliver their political goals. They want 'impact', which comes with the challenges discussed above. The largest backer of European venture capital is the EU's European Investment Fund. It provides 20–30% of the venture capital raised on the continent. For Europe's VCs, it is something of a Faustian bargain, because in contrast to the US supply-side stimulus, demand-side funding by the state has a tendency to come with constraints (even if they are innocuous absurdities, like trying to quantify potential or measure 'impact').

But there are signs that the tone of things is changing in Europe, in bizarre ways. The recent pullback of US military funding from Europe has seen an upsurge in the potential for defence-led support for new tech. How much of this will be channelled into venture capital or the usual big contractors is another question, but early signs are promising. Venture investment into European defence start-ups has increased fivefold so far this decade. Meanwhile, NATO and the UK have both recently established their own defence-related venture capital funds in move that echo America's highly successful and long-standing DARPA programme.

It's quite the ideological departure from Europe's historic insistence on 'environmental, social, governance' requirements. Ironically, it will most likely be many of the same companies and technologies being funded. An AI company working on climate change can often be the same people and tech that now pivots to work on the modern battlefield. It's not cynical, it's just entrepreneurial business responding to what the market demands. It just so happens that the early adopter for deep technologies is very often the state.

Even woke consultancies like McKinsey, which have been pushing ESG investment for years, are now advising European start-ups on how they could learn from the United States and capitalise on Europe's war fever. Its first tip is for policymakers to invest in propaganda to ensure the public favours war. Their second tip speaks to my point above about impact:

> Many start-ups struggle to secure VC and growth investment due to regulatory requirements and limited pools of potential capital. For example, limited partner investors – both public and private – often prohibit investments in lethal or purely military technologies. By addressing the challenges that cause these investment constraints, available capital could be expanded, and the ecosystem growth could be accelerated[2].

It almost makes me want to change my mind about the value of ESG platitudes. There will, no doubt, be rich profits in catering to European defence aspirations, but it's not what is usually meant by 'creative destruction'.

Creative Destruction in the Economy

The economist Joseph Schumpeter came up with his concept of creative destruction in the 1940s after a close reading of Marx, except, by contrast to the father of *destructive-destruction*, rather than being against it, Schumpeter saw it as a necessary and natural process – not a manifesto for action but a simple description of how reality works. But the Marxist sentiment has never fully died away, and protectionist politicians remain very wary of this aspect of venture capital, which is arguably the most conspicuous force for organised creative destruction in the modern economy.

Of course, creative destruction *is* a natural process, and it happens across the economy all the time, in a billion different budget decisions, behind boardroom and state-room doors, which takes resources from one department or division and gives them to another. The difference here is that such an optimal allocation of resources is venture capital's *raison d'être* – it is fully committed to the possibility of making things better, while harbouring no allegiance to vested interests. So if you want to back a barbarian, you need to face this reality and be prepared to benefit from it. You must be committed to the sacrifice of dead wood in favour of new growth. And no matter how you invest, you will be doing this: you can invest in a renewable energy fund and make a coal miner jobless. Or impoverish a taxi driver by backing a fund that invests in a ride-hailing app. In this world, you are either on the side of painful progress or slow decay. *War is the father of all things*, said Heraclitus. It's not an aspiration; it's just an observation.

Let's take an extreme example of creative destruction, a company most will know: Uber.

In the early days of gunpowder and musketry, warriors of the Scottish Highlands developed a battle tactic that was so gutsy and unexpected that it sowed terror in the hearts of their enemies long after it had ceased to be an effective ruse. It was called 'the Highland charge', and it involved waiting for the first volley from the enemy and then simply charging full pelt towards them as they desperately tried to reload.

Uber's go-to-market strategy was effectively an all-out assault on multiple jurisdictions in an internationally coordinated attack that had policymakers scrabbling for the rule book. Uber's very business model was a slap in the face to some of the most highly politicised rules that exist. Their tactics actively side-stepped rules, obeying the letter and trampling on the spirit. And sometimes not even the letter. They developed a secret software app called Greyball to identify and exclude customers they suspected were government officials or inspectors. They sabotaged rivals. They declared their drivers were contractors, not employees. They labelled cars with their brand without owning them. They didn't need to invent GPS – the US government had done that. They just used it as a scheduling assistant. They arranged subprime loans so drivers could afford cars. They spent millions on targeted lobbying. And today, almost everyone, whether they were on the side of the regulated taxi industry or not, hails a ride with a tap, without a second's thought.

Uber was basically a ballsy, well-capitalised Highland charge and only venture capital could have made it work. Private equity, while structurally similar, would have failed the company on almost every aspect of its due diligence, including its thickest of red lines: regulatory compliance. Or imagine an IPO roadshow: *we are setting up a business to flout the regulations of dozens of countries and jeopardise the livelihoods of high-profile workers*. It was only after the dirty work was done that the public market investor was allowed to buy in.

Uber was exceptional, even for venture capital, in its aggression. I simply use it to drive home the point that bringing anything new into this world is, in the abstract, a beautiful experience, full of promise and hope and ribbons of joy. In reality, it's a bloody mess, a screaming rage attack that will leave deep scars no matter how full of love and good intentions you are. Venture capital, and indeed the entire scientific-atomic endeavour, is based on the belief that striving for progress, while painful, will ultimately prove better for humanity than the alternative.

The Precautionary Principle

At the same time, you don't have to be a Luddite to be concerned that we could be rushing headlong into a techno-dystopia via well-capitalised, unconstrained experimentation. It's very easy to get cynical about progress in a world where children are hooked on social media, modern medicine creates viruses that it then sells the vaccines for and where artificial intelligence takes your job and then has the audacity to do it better.

'Make something people want' may seem a banal refrain, but the social impact of cutting-edge innovation is starting to look somewhat disconnected from this. Meanwhile, the pattern of innovation in deep tech is no less concerning. The Silicon Valley credo of 'move fast and break things' is not the greatest PR motto.

Even so, on balance, I prefer technological innovation in the profit-motivated hands of venture capitalists than with the state. For instance, I am aware of nothing in the venture capital world so reckless as the US and Chinese government funded gain-of-function biopharmaceutical research, that gave us Covid-19. Or the UK and US governments' quiet experiment to geo-engineer the planet by dimming the sun[i].

I say all this because much venture capital fund marketing are claims about impact – but context is everything, and the only way to get a feel for that impact is to look at the details.

Impact in Context

To understand the ethos and real-world impact of venture investment, there is no shortcut for looking at real-world stories. Here is one of my favourites.

When he was five years old, Douglas Anderson's son had spontaneous retinal detachment that went undetected. He eventually had surgery, partly to check the condition of his other eye – the

---

[i] In 2023, University College London called one of its geo-engineering projects SATAN: Stratospheric Aerosol Transport and Nucleation. It's reminiscent of China's national surveillance network that its engineers named Skynet, after the AI in *The Terminator*.

only way to determine risk. The surgery failed to save the sight of his bad eye, and no notes were taken about his good eye. The boy underwent years of follow-ups, but the surgeons could tell them very little. Douglas discovered there had been no diagnostic innovations in ophthalmology for 50 years.

He spent fruitless years searching for ways to make disease in the eye more visible, and at the end, he threw his last few shekels at a long-shot idea. 'People said it was a worthless idea, it wouldn't work, and it would be too expensive even if it did', he told me. 'Over several years, we were turned down by almost every venture capitalist in the UK, North America and Europe at least once. Except one'.

Anne Glover was CEO of a UK venture firm called Amadeus. 'When I first met Douglas, his "bench demonstrator" was a ping-pong ball and a laser. He said, imagine this is the eyeball. . .' The fact that there had been no innovation in ophthalmology for half a century was both worrying and encouraging. Amadeus invested and, as is usually the case in venture capital, did so in stages – five times over the course of several years. These are called investment 'rounds' or 'series', and they are 'milestone' investments, tied to the performance of the company – but that performance is typically highly subjective. Since nearly all early-stage companies miss their financial plans, the decision is based on judgement not calculation. Each tranche is an independent decision, with every effort taken to avoid the sunk-cost fallacy.

By the end, the company, Optos, was building machines that gave a complete field of view. The machines were a massive diagnostic breakthrough and went on to save the sight of millions of people. It went on to list on the main market of the London Stock Exchange, providing an exit and big return for Amadeus.

During the course of the venture, Douglas would tell Anne he wanted his machines to be ubiquitous. Anne would tell Douglas she needed them to be profitable. Only by coming together and putting profit first and impact as the destination did they both achieve their goals.

By the way, when his son was 20, he lost sight in his other eye. They took him to hospital, where they had an Optos machine. It diagnosed the problem before the surgeon arrived and paved the way to successful restoration.

The Future Is Bright

If investment is an expression of hope and optimism that, through sacrifice and effort, we can do 'more with less' and constantly improve the human condition, then venture capital is at the vanguard of investment. The next big thing is not on the stock market. It might be in a lab somewhere, or in someone's garage or brain, but it's unlikely to ever make an impact in the world without the support of well-organised and capitalised individuals who believe in it. That is the venture capital industry.

Such is the rate of disruption today, primarily wrought by AI, that being invested in a market that specialises in that disruption might be one of the safest places to be. Honestly, I wonder how half the people I know (particularly the lawyers) will make a living in five years' time – it won't be how they do it today, that's for sure. In such circumstances, embracing the disruption might be the only viable option.

The venture capital ecosystem will not be immune to this disruption. How might it evolve? There are clues.

In the United States, we are seeing the big Silicon Valley VCs, such as Sequoia, Andreesen Horowitz and Lightspeed, change their regulatory status to allow them to move beyond investing in start-up equity. It could be that AI disruption is so profound that they seek to bring company development more in-house, as semi-incubators. They could go the other way and invest in public equities that are on the verge of disruption and so start to push their buyout cousins from their classical territory. They could create a longer term venture ecosystem by acquiring secondary start-up stock and effectively allow innovative companies to stay in private hands for longer – or forever. And if they can position themselves as the corporate AI puppet masters, their own value as venture capital management companies will become immense, making themselves strong candidates for a public listing. This is definitely a trend to watch. The good thing about investing in listed venture capital managers (which we will look at more closely in Chapter 7) is that you would get exposure to both the fee income of the fund manager and the performance of their underlying funds, which means you are strongly aligned.

More than any other part of the private markets – or even the wider investment world – venture capital has the potential to turbocharge your investment returns.

But it's also an area that really calls for diversification.

For those 'accredited' investors tempted to invest directly into a venture capital fund, it's worth remembering that building a properly diversified portfolio of such commitments will get expensive, quickly. At tickets of $100k, even if you only invested in two funds per year over the course of five years, that's still a $2m commitment for the venture capital part of your portfolio that might be 3–5% of your total. For the majority, various listed and unlisted feeder funds, outlined at the end of this chapter and explained in more detail in Part 3, will be a better option.

And in general, I would say the less money you have, the more important cheap access to diversified exposure will be. I'm wary of the growing trend of retail investors being invited to commit directly to (mainly US) venture capital funds, often ones that have partnered with B-list celebrities and sports stars to attract people, with a low minimum ticket size (say, $500) that can be bought using an app. This is not the type of brand-name credibility that would attract a serious investor. Beware borrowed status.

Venture as a Career

If you are the type of person attracted to venture capital as an investment, you probably have some entrepreneurial flair, perhaps even scalable, digital competencies. One way to get frontline exposure to this form of barbarianism is to work for a venture capital backed start-up. Unlike in private equity, where co-investment is normally confined to the senior management, in start-ups and scale-ups, the way they attract talent is through equity ownership or options. Your financial risk will be highly concentrated, your potential upside will be life-changing. More to the point, you will be exposed to a career-development environment that can't be replicated in the corporate world. They say venture years are like dog years – because you learn so much, about yourself, about business and all parts of business, given that early employees need to 'muck in' in areas outside their own competencies. Even if it doesn't ultimately pay out, there is no such thing as failure in the venture world – that's just not the mindset of this industry. The failure to venture forth, to give it a go – that is the only disqualifier. Everything else is upside – whether in the form of dollars or experience.

For insight into specific funds that provide exposure to venture capital, and that are available for investment by qualifying individual investors, scan this QR code.

7

The Rise of Free Banks

'The first sign of civilisation is not the plough or the forge, but the contract of debt'.

– David Graeber

Ron Paul, the American author and politician, has called power over money supply 'the most sought-after monopolistic power of man'. The more centralised the state or overextended the sovereign, the greater the temptation to de-privatise credit and centrally plan money through the crown.

By contrast, in free societies, money-lending is more of a 'peer-to-peer' or merchant-to-merchant affair. Individuals, families, temples and guilds would lend money, individually or more often as part of a consortium, and over time, the most successful became international banks. These banks were typically private partnerships controlled by dynasties – like the Rothschilds, the Medicis and the Barings. This meant they bore their own risk and as such their lending was biased on the side of prudence and based on judgements about individual creditors. 'A man I do not trust could not get money from me on all the bonds in Christendom', said John Pierpont Morgan.

The past century has been a conspicuous example of control and centralisation of credit, with the establishment of (once-controversial) central banks and the move from the gold standard to fiat-money creation. State-sponsored and regulated banks have effectively had a chokehold on the supply of credit.

This detachment from the free market is bad for borrowers and removes 'skin in the game' for lenders. By the turn of the millennium, implicitly state-sponsored bank CEOs were less likely to equate simple moral virtues, such as good faith and prudence, with commercial success. They considered themselves rational optimisers and instruments of the Market. 'While the music plays, we must keep dancing', said the CEO of the world's largest bank (at the time), on the eve of the Global Financial Crisis.

The modern era of state-backed banking emerged gradually, in response to the crises of the Great Depression and World War II. To protect savers from losses and bank runs, the US government introduced deposit insurance and gave the state a central role in finance. But this safety net dulled market discipline: banks could take greater risks under an implicit state guarantee. The break with gold in the early 1970s pushed the system further. Once bank lending no longer required a finite monetary backing, credit creation became the engine of fiat money supply, giving banks access to cheap capital and central bank liquidity. The result was a system of centralised monetary control and artificially low interest rates.

Few people worried about this, because the benefits appeared to be so great. For instance, it lubricated the development of a vast and impersonal capital market. In stark contrast to the merchant lending practices of old, these capital markets focused on efficiency and scale, using standardised bond offerings that could be bought and traded rapidly. But such standardisation meant that only the most stable creditors qualified – typically sovereigns and very large companies. Such credits are known as 'investment-grade', because they are low-risk. Unfortunately, they also tend to be very low return, and sometimes they offer no real return at all – hardly what ordinary people would consider *worthy of investment*. More to the point, it's hardly the stuff of dynamic economic development either. After all, it does not tend to be governments and monopolies that create wealth. Rather, it is the risk-takers in the real enterprise economy – precisely those excluded from the shiny capital markets.

If you look closely enough at today's debt capital markets issuance, you'll notice that an enormous amount of capital flow is related to the incessant financial manoeuvring and liability management of giant bureaucracies and financial entities – little of which has a clear relationship with productive capital for investment. It is what Austrian economists would call malinvestment: artificially cheap credit causing a misallocation of resources into unproductive and unsustainable projects. Take the pandemic lockdown years of 2021–2022 – these were an absolute bonanza on the debt capital markets – as the world's economic engine ground to a halt, investment bankers and financial services intermediaries hit the jackpot, smashing all-time high fee-income records. It's not a great sign when capital markets have such a strongly inverse relationship to productive activity.

The reality is that large companies don't really need much external capital. Most have more than enough profits to fund any extra capital investment, but instead, as corporate profits have soared over the decades, corporate investment has fallen.

Given that the whole capital market system was underwritten by state-sponsored banks on the basis of an artificially low cost of capital, the system has been somewhat akin to robbing Peter to pay Paul. Those getting robbed were those furthest away from the new money creation, bond auctions and asset-ownership (people living hand-to-mouth on salaries) and those that got paid were those closest to it (financial industry participants).[i]

In an ultimately futile attempt to mitigate this 'moral hazard' (where banks could externalise their risk and privatise their gains), a vast regulatory apparatus was then put in place, and after successive banking crises, this framework became ever more complex. But the result was precisely the opposite of its stated intention – to protect ordinary savers – a fact that reached its apogee with the bank bailouts of 2009. Every 'asset-lite' citizen has been paying the price ever since.

The one good thing (you might say) about the GFC was that, unlike the many smaller crises that led to the same system being propped up by more rules, it prompted a genuine rethink. The result was that banks were forced to become much more conservative in their lending practices (via international rules such as Basel III). Now that their chokehold on lending had been broken, the free market could now compete for real economy lending. The purpose of the regulation was to make banks safer rather than to encourage the emergence of a private market. But that's what happened. And investor capital has flowed in like the breaking of a dam.

By 2017, just six years after the implementation of Basel III, the private credit markets were already worth $700bn. By 2024, the figure had

---

[i] A phenomenon known as 'the Cantillon Effect'.

ballooned to $1.7trn, and it is on track to reach $3trn by the end of 2025. Some put the addressable market for private credit at $30trn in the United States alone.[1] The scale is colossal and dwarfs the size potential of private equity. (There were even some rumours that a so-called Basel Endgame would raise bank capital requirements even further, which would have all but ended their competitive position in wholesale lending markets, but after some lobbying work – *who else will fund the green transition?* – this prospect seems more remote.)

With bank credit more expensive, corporate borrowers are now looking for better deals elsewhere. Meanwhile, lenders can operate on the basis of a cost of capital that is more reflective of investor risk and appetite. As a result, institutional investors have been piling in. For instance, US state pensions have increased their allocation to private credit from 2.8% in 2021 to 4.4% in 2024.[2]

To be sure, private credit is still part of a very centralised monetary system, and it is just as exposed to central bank architecture and influence. But it is less prone to the gigantism and too-big-to-fail moral hazard of the old system. This has positive implications for real-economy lending. For nearly a century, the business of lending to the world's true value creators – middle market companies, infrastructure projects, start-ups, farmers and growers – has been a tiny investment market, populated by a few mavericks operating at the margins of the economy. Now, with regulation that finally treats deposit-taking banks as the utilities they actually are, we are witnessing something approximating a step towards a re-privatisation of credit itself, starting with the partial disintermediation of banks. The scale of the opportunity is vast.

The Great Credit Land-grab

Private equity tends to get all the headlines but from the perspective of 'going mainstream', it has a constraining factor: it's not very scalable. Despite its rapid growth in recent decades, the total assets managed by private equity firms globally are still less than half the size of BlackRock. That's because the hands-on, bottom-up nature of private equity ownership, which is the basis of its success, also consigns it to relatively linear growth.

By contrast, private credit is, by its nature, both a much larger and more rapidly scalable opportunity. As such, in recent years, the development of private credit has been furious and unrelenting. But it's not a simple story of private credit funds stealing market share from traditional banking brands (although that is definitely happening). Even though the GFC was a generation ago, the credit markets are just too vast and the revolution has been too sudden to allow for a gradual emergence of an orderly private credit industry that can take over all the functions of the traditional banking and wholesale lending markets.

Instead, we've seen a burst of innovation, from start-ups and native private credit firms, private equity and buyout groups expanding across the capital structure, big investment banks repackaging private credit, fintechs and speciality lenders colonising niches, plus a steady stream of joint ventures and partnership announcements among all of the above. It's an all-out land-grab and everyone is jostling for position across credit markets as diverse as leverage loans, aircraft leasing, commercial real estate, infrastructure and consumer lending.

At the same time, we are seeing an electronification of credit markets, which sounds very retro, but bond offerings remain surprisingly analogue affairs. They are not arranged 'over-the-counter' exactly, but via something called a telephone. Even the wealthiest individual investors never get *that* call. But increasingly, such credit products are trading online, which threatens to marginalise traditional banks further. (This all happened in the equity and macro markets a long time ago.)

If this revolution was happening in a more familiar sector, it would never be out of the press. Only a mystic would claim to know what the credit market will look like in a decade from now. But if the past quarter-century belonged to private equity, it looks likely that private credit will be the major growth asset-class of the next 25 years.

Middle-market Lending

The backbone of today's private credit market is 'sponsor-backed' lending – financing provided to private equity firms to support leveraged buyouts, recapitalisations and bolt-on acquisitions. In these transactions, the private equity sponsor is the 'real' client of the credit fund, and the deal structures, covenants and leverage levels are largely shaped by the sponsor's acquisition plan. In effect, private credit has stepped into the role once occupied by the syndicated leveraged loan and high-yield bond markets, but in a more concentrated and less intermediated way.

There is also a growing segment of 'direct-to-company' lending that looks more like old-style merchant banking. These are situations where credit funds make loans directly to companies – often those too small, too idiosyncratic or too time-sensitive for the public debt markets – and craft terms that fit the borrower's specific needs. Here, the credit fund's real differentiator is the ability to make individual judgements, conduct deep diligence and tailor loan structures, rather than relying on the formulaic approaches and credit scoring of traditional banks or the standardised terms of the bond market.

Because this kind of bottom-up work is resource-intensive, private credit funds often specialise by sector or type of loan – from distressed situations and 'venture debt' to mid-market facilities and even large-cap deals. They may provide junior capital such as second-lien or mezzanine debt, safer senior loans or hybrids like 'unitranche' facilities. These bespoke corners of the market coexist alongside and are in many ways enabled by the massive flow of sponsor-driven LBO financing that defines private credit today.

But it's not all one-way traffic. For instance, revolving credit facilities do not work from a private credit context, since they tie up capital without offering a yield. Banks use this as a carrot and a stick for borrowers by making (low-margin) revolvers contingent on a wider financing package. It's a similar story with just-in-time finance, such as short-term working capital and trade finance. For now, private credit has the edge where speed, certainty and complexity collide. They can also be more flexible and specific in their covenants and terms and can be more aggressive in the leverage levels. But how the competitive landscape will eventually play out remains a known unknown.

Financing the Private Equity Funds Themselves

As well as financing private equity backed companies, private credit firms also provide loan facilities for the funds themselves. This is a rapidly evolving opportunity as general partners push against the constraints and inefficiencies of the limited partnership structure.

For instance, subscription lines or 'capital call facilities' are short-term loans that are secured against LP commitments, and private equity managers use them to bridge the gap between calling capital from LPs and making an investment. Such 'equity bridge' finance is a cash management tool (but it can also shorten the time an LP's capital is put to work).

Another similar product is NAV credit lines that are secured by the value of the portfolio and can be used to finance distributions when exits are scarce and LPs want some cash back or to finance investment within the portfolio.

From an LP perspective, such practices can be controversial because they can skew the alignment of interest between the GP and LP – on which the very success of private equity is based. For instance, sub-lines can artificially boost the return metric used to calculate carried interest, known as IRRs.

Looking at such tactics, you might say, no inheritance is so great that it is immune to despoilment. But there's another way of looking at it. Conventions have value, but they must be combined with innovation if a market is to adapt, experiment and be anti-fragile. Some such innovations will be cyclical and die away. Others will become incorporated into the structure of the market. As a barbarian investor, diversified across the capital structure – including credit – you can be in a position to capture value from every corner of the private markets.

While private equity is familiar territory for many private credit players (historically, culturally, sometimes organisationally), private equity is just the very tip of private credit's iceberg of opportunity.

The Great Convergence

The monster consumer credit market is the next on the radar for disruption, along with the asset-based finance market, which is debt backed by contractual cash flows based on a defined pool of assets, and includes auto loans, credit cards and mortgages, as well as more niche areas such as music back catalogues and aircraft leasing.

This really is outside the traditional stomping ground of most private capital managers and perhaps that's why we are seeing some unusual tie-ups between them and traditional banks. And this isn't the only disruption happening in consumer finance. We are also seeing plucky little fintechs sweep in and catch the attention of the average app user. The problem is that few, if any institutions, have all the capabilities, experience and relationships in-house to bring it all together.

This is prompting some intriguing manoeuvres. Take, for instance, a 2024 joint venture between private markets manager the Carlyle Group and Citibank. The partnership is aimed at jointly backing fintech companies that are focused on asset-based finance. The duo plans to co-invest in these start-ups, and then in the consumer loans that are originated by the fintechs. (In a further conflation, it will actually be Citi's venture capital team that will be helping sift through the start-up ecosystem.) Eventually, these loans can be bundled, securitised and sold as public bonds, presumably drawing on Citi's infrastructure in this area.

Ultimately, what we are seeing is not some big showdown or competition between traditional banks and private market newcomers, but – as one would expect of a free market – specialisation, where each participant-type plays to their competitive advantage, often by cooperating as part of a sophisticated specialist ecosystem.

For instance, banks appear to be positioning to take on a prime broker-type role, where they become strategic partners or even service providers to a more distributed banking system. In this new system, credit funds become the main holders of debt-risk (the role typically associated with the word 'bank'). Meanwhile, the traditional banks become service providers to them, arranging fund finance solutions (like subscription lines, warehousing, GP financing); origination and distribution services (like syndicating loans and structuring CLOs, thus allowing them to maintain their client relationships); back-office securities services, as well as trading and hedging, particularly as a secondaries market for private credit gets going.

For the end-investor on the product side, some believe this will effectively look like a great convergence between public and private forms of credit. But it will actually be more like a reverse takeover, as private credit managers take the whip hand and choose the distribution vehicles that suit their purposes. For instance, they may wish to wrap up illiquid loans into mortgage-backed securities or CLOs, allowing investors to capture the value-creation benefits of commitment.

Having said all this, it's unwise to be too enthusiastic about the prospects for lending at any particular moment in time. So long as we have central banks, credit will be highly cyclical, and there are always players that find ways to hide financial risk in complex structures. But there is intense competition and diversity in today's credit market, and it's largely backed by equity rather than by ever more leverage.

Real Assets Loans

Private real assets include real estate, infrastructure, utilities and natural resources, and these represent a huge opportunity for private credit. Again, there are push and pull factors. Western governments have become so indebted and subsumed by healthcare and defence expenditure that they are no longer prepared to maintain the fundamental infrastructure of modern states, let alone invest in major upgrades.

And these upgrades are long overdue. Mario Draghi's famous 2024 report on European competitiveness recommended a minimum annual investment of €800bn, or 5% of the bloc's GDP, if it is to close the yawning gap between the European Union and the United States and China. Meanwhile, the United States faces a rapidly ageing infrastructure of roads, bridges, sewers, ports and that's before we get on to the upgrades required to meet 21st century demands of new energy systems and technological infrastructure – not least the power-hungry data centres required to support the advancement of AI.

The good news is that such assets are a good match for private credit portfolios, given their stable, predictable cashflows, which are often inflation-linked (their income responds to inflation). They also offer significantly more attractive yields than, say investing in 'investment-grade' corporate bonds (often several percentage points better for comparably rated credits). And such assets are intrinsically less volatile, even in the context of private markets generally.

In real estate, private markets funds are buying up and lending against properties as diverse as residential housing, old people's homes, commercial real estate, industrial and logistics land, retail and agriculture. These tend to be structured as asset-based loans, and these accounted for about 40% of private credit in 2024 – a figure that is likely to grow rapidly.[3]

In addition, these privately arranged loans are increasingly pushing up into areas of the lending market still dominated by banks and the capital markets: namely, very large deals, securitisations and investment-grade lending.

In infrastructure, for instance funds are able to take the time to understand complex assets or project finance requirements and to arrange bespoke loan facilities that rival what even the ultra-efficient capital markets can offer. These are structured to provide investors with a higher return than comparably rated bonds, plus a floating-rate yield that offers less volatility.

The Evolution of Credit Funds

The structure favoured by most private credit lenders is the classic closed-ended LP fund that we have encountered many times before. But the terms of these vehicles differ. Management fees are typically around

1% compared to nearly double that in private equity. (The lower down the capital structure – i.e. the closer to the equity, such as mezzanine or distressed debt – and the more complex the strategy, the higher the fee.) The manager's carried interest is typically 10% rather than 20% in private equity, but the hurdle is a little lower, typically 5% rather than 8%.

Free-market Money for a Safer World

One should be wary of innovation in finance. As one central banker reasonably said, the last good financial innovation was the ATM. Ironically enough, central banks themselves are a somewhat recent innovation of disputed benefit. By contrast, private credit is not novel; it is a reversion to the system of free-market money that built modern civilisation. While one must be forever watchful, at a structural level, the rise of private credit has very positive implications for the resilience of the financial system itself.

There can never be a 'bank-run' on a private credit fund. That's because private credit is funded by equity. If this sounds counter-intuitive, it's only because you've spent so long 'through the looking glass'. A banking system that relies on financial leverage via the creation of short-term debt and maturity transformation is (demonstrably) a recipe for perpetual catastrophe and immoral risk transfer. By contrast, a credit system backed by fully consenting equity investors who rightly adopt the full measure of risk and reward is the only basis for a well-functioning, fair and anti-fragile financial system. Austrian School economists would recognise the emergence of private credit funds as equivalent to free banks – the 100% reserve banks envisaged by Murray Rothbard, which do not engage in the sleight of hand that is fractional reserve banking (the lending out of the same money multiple times) which gives rise to the business cycle. Instead, they are private pools of capital backed by fully consenting investors, not unwitting depositors.

This renaissance of private credit markets also means that anyone can enjoy the fruits of prudent, productive lending, not just the elite. Today, anybody with capital and patience can do as the Rothschild family or the Barings or the Medicis. Diversified money-lending is now open to the everyday barbarian, those who have slipped the yoke of centralised, standardised public markets, and who receive real cash that flows from financing productive activity in the real economy.

The true risks in this revived system are something like the opposite of what you might read in the media. Let me explain.

A vast regulatory apparatus has been established to regulate the moral hazard of state-sponsored banks. All those individuals now have very little to keep them occupied. Inevitably, they will start looking at private credit. The same applies to law firms, whose large regulatory teams rely on an ever more complex rule book to keep up the billable hours. I receive regular updates from law firms 'predicting' how the SEC might look to increase its oversight of private credit, in missives that appear almost like wish fulfilment. This loose and unholy alliance between regulator and law firm goes like this: the law firm advises that their clients begin to 'manage' 'risks' that they 'believe' the regulator is looking at, like 'valuation challenges' for instance. Over time, these risk-management processes become 'best-practice' and must therefore be upheld and enshrined in legislation.

In some walks of life, AI cannot come fast enough.

The Original Bond Villain

The 1980s saw the birth of the high yield bond market. Michael Milken, who we encountered in Chapter 3, ignited something like a guerrilla assault on the rarefied corporate bond markets by arranging and selling securities beneath the contempt of state-coddled banks and public markets. Derided as 'junk bonds', these instruments offered compelling returns and helped fuel the first wave of LBOs. While they were still publicly-traded securities, many see Milken as the spiritual father of today's private credit market.

Before this, bonds could only be issued by governments and the bluest of blue-chip companies, which were considered 'investment-grade' – as if such entities were the only creditors worth lending to. In reality, investment-grade means low-yield – and sometimes even a loss, once inflation is factored in. The fact that such products can be marketed as unimpeachable investment propositions speaks volumes about the warped conception of risk in modern regulated markets.

Milken's bold foray inevitably made him a target. For activities that, even in white-collar terms, were very minor, he was sentenced to 10 years in prison and a lifetime ban from the securities industry. Compare this to how the establishment protected its own during the Global Financial Crisis. Milken's real crime, of course, was to satisfy free-market demand in a centrally stage-managed market. It was an act of barbarism against an empire.

Milken is now a philanthropist who is treated with quiet respect by the leaders of Wall Street. His activities legitimised the high-yield credit market, which powered most US LBOs, and paved the way for a freer market in credit itself.

The rebirth of private credit funds is nothing less than a return to real banking – the kind that our merchant forebears would recognise. Credit funds and CLOs are banks in the truest sense of the word. They are not the lame 'non-banks' of regulatory taxonomy, nor the sinister 'shadow banks' of journalistic prose. Those labels are designed to obscure the fact that these institutions perform the honest risk-taking that 20th century banking abandoned. What passes as 'banking' today is little more than state-sponsored counterfeiting.

For too long, the best investment opportunities have been captured by the fiat cartel, big corporations and governments, operating in rarefied global capital markets, while individuals were relegated to the role of depositor, consumer or taxpayer. Today, thanks to a newly minted private credit market, every citizen with sufficient patience and capital can, if they choose, take on the risk and reward of free-market banking.

For insight into specific funds and companies that provide exposure to private credit that are available for investment by qualifying individual investors, scan this QR code.

Part III

Access

In this final part, we look at how you can invest like a barbarian, and even how you can become one yourself.

Whichever strategy appeals to you, there is a crucial question you must now address. . . What type of vehicle will you use to access the market?

Broadly, the options are:

Vehicle Type

1. **Classical closed-end 'LP' fund**
   Commit directly to closed-end fund partnerships

2. **Gated evergreens**
   Commit to an open-ended, illiquid fund

3. **Listed private capital company**
   Invest in closed-end private markets 'stocks'

There is no 'right' way to approach the markets – your choice will depend on your circumstances and personal preferences. It's worth noting that just because some avenues are only open to the wealthiest investors, this does not necessarily make them 'better'. Indeed, many institutional investors choose to access the market through universal entry access mechanisms.

In Chapter 8, we look at the prospect of investing in classic closed-ended funds. The entry price of doing so is falling, making this a viable option for a whole new class of affluent investors. In Chapter 9, we look at a relatively novel feeder fund structure, the gated evergreen, perpetual vehicles with even lower entry prices.

I would argue such approaches to private markets are a more serious undertaking than investments in trading markets because they usually require a commitment – by which I mean an obligation over time that will be costly to renege upon. In fact, I would go further and say that such commitment is what constitutes an investment – anything else is just trading and speculation. How can you say you are truly invested in something when you have reserved the right to sell at a moment's notice or less? And what message does that send to the agents who are managing your so-called investment? And yet this world of publicly traded assets is the one that has infected the broader consciousness, and the one that is, for many, considered synonymous with 'investment', and the benchmark against which we judge all else.

Making investments in the real world takes time because creating value also takes time. But it doesn't need to be your time. That's one of the beauties of commitment. You free yourself from the burden of perpetual doubt, of second-guessing yourself, of keeping your options open, of changing your mind. And at the same time, you provide those who take your hard-earned cash and apply their labour to it with sufficient certainty to do worthwhile things with your capital. It's a very simple and ancient solution to a timeless problem.

In Chapter 10, we look at listed private equity – an idea that, superficially at least, seems to contradict the case made for private markets thus far. But public and private markets should not be antagonistic, and there is a strong case to be made that only by combining the best of these markets can investors have their cake and eat it.

Even so, for those mostly familiar with stock markets, private markets require something of a mindset shift. That's because the foundational concepts of modern investment, such as return, risk and value, have become highly eccentric in public markets investment theory. For instance, return has come to be considered as merely the performance of an investment relative to an abstract benchmark; risk is viewed merely as relative fluctuations of prices; meanwhile, value is a concept that has become almost incomprehensible.

As we shall see, in private markets, these terms mean pretty much what ordinary people think they mean: return is what you get back; risk is the chance of failure; and value is a highly subjective, almost poetic concept that will always be in the eye of the beholder. This is the subject of Chapter 11.

Chapter 12 will look at how you can become a barbarian yourself, by having a career in or around the private capital industry, or even by setting up your own firm and raising a fund.

And finally, we will look at the likely effect on the wider world of private markets activity.

For more insight into how to access private markets and the trend of democratisation, scan this QR code.

8

Fully Committed

'How poor are they that have not patience!'
— **William Shakespeare**

Investing directly into traditional closed-end private markets funds as an 'LP'-style investor is no longer the preserve of the super-rich. There are online investment platforms that provide access to top funds for as little as $25k to $50k, and in some jurisdictions, funds are offering access for a fraction of this.

But even if you can, in theory, invest in private markets through this classic fund structure – *should you*? Your decision may be based on hard logic and financial concerns only, or it may reflect your personal tastes and family circumstances.

When investing these types of sums, most people will do so through a trusted intermediary, who can help find the vehicle type that works for them. Even for those with the financial resources, managing a programme of traditional closed-ended fund investment is not a trivial exercise.

'If you have a client with a $5m net worth and wants to allocate, say, 5–10% to private markets, it's not that easy', explains Cyril Demaria, Affiliate Professor at the EDHEC Business School, and Head of Private Markets Strategy at Julius Bar. 'You will want to diversify over time, by strategy, by industry and then perhaps, by manager. So you start to have a matrix, where you must combine these constraints. The amount of available capital could quickly become a limitation. But the good news is, we now have more tools to support this capital deployment'.

In addition, he tells me that expanding this access to individuals is still a learning process for all concerned – from the fund manager through to the end-investor – and private wealth managers sit in the middle of this dynamic.

The investment decision will be influenced by the individual's time horizon. For older clients, they may be less willing to 'lock up' their capital for long periods – unless they are taking a multi-generational view of wealth. Younger wealthy people may be more willing to take the longer-term perspective.

Another factor is the background of the investor. If they made their wealth in the corporate world, perhaps they will be most comfortable with mainstream buyouts and private credit. If they are entrepreneurs, perhaps they will have more appetite for venture capital.

The financial adviser will also need to consider the extent to which the client wishes to be involved in decisions – the level of ongoing involvement and complexity they are willing to tolerate. For some, the cash flow from directly investing into closed-end funds is worth the level of involvement – and nothing can replace this flow of hard cash. For others, operational simplicity will make 'evergreen'-type structures preferable.

There is no single answer or even (as yet) a formula for determining the optimal profile. On top of this, the committed nature of the asset class creates an inertia that will need to be recognised and managed. Private market portfolios are like oil tankers that can only be turned very slowly.

Another question to consider: what should be your allocation to private markets as a proportion of your investable assets? Around 20% has become fairly standard for institutional investors, while some endowments go as high as 40% or more. The longer your investment time horizon and the greater your ability to lock capital away for the future, the larger might be your private markets allocation. The bias has always been that endowments are the longest horizon investors, pension funds next, then insurers and corporations and last of all, individuals. But as universities frantically check behind the proverbial sofa in their dash for cash, and many pension funds continue to act like day traders on the stock markets, family office managers are endlessly asked to sell assets so some uncle can buy a new villa. I think there is a case that this entire paradigm is upside down. There are an awful lot of quietly wealthy, prudent people out there who want to invest for the future, for their family and for a legacy. They could be the bedrock of private markets.

Where do private markets sit?

How should you categorise and contextualise your private markets allocation? Again, there is no single correct answer. You might view private equity as sitting alongside public equity in the capital appreciation bucket, and private credit alongside your fixed income allocation. Or you might categorise assets by their liquidity profile.

Divorce and Commitments

Of course, life happens. And one thing that can happen in life is divorce. There is an old, slightly tortured observation that the average life of a private markets fund is longer than the average marriage. Thankfully this is an exaggeration, but it is worth considering the added complexity of dealing with illiquid assets and ongoing commitments in such a scenario. Matrimonial assets must usually be split equally, and it is typically the most convoluted and hotly disputed part of the negotiation. There may be ongoing funding requirements, confidentiality concerns and a much trickier task around valuation.

Lois Rogers, who advises private equity investors and their spouses in divorce proceedings, says that observing the clean break principle can be tricky when it comes to closed-ended private markets fund commitments. 'If the couple are young, there might not be enough cash or alternative assets to compensate', she says. In this case, the spouse can end up waiting five or ten years, during which time the barbarian must provide information about valuations and so on. A recent case in the United Kingdom saw two expert witnesses coming up with vastly different valuations for a private equity investment. A year later, the husband received a distribution that was 10 times larger than he had expected. This is particularly tricky for fund managers who are invested in their own funds and are subject to confidentiality agreements. 'For individual investors entering the asset class through more liquid structures, this will be easier', says Lois, 'because they can just pass on information with no confidentiality concerns – both investors will be passive'.

Public Pension Fund Exposure

If you hold a defined benefit pension, it is quite possible that you already have direct exposure to classic closed-ended private markets funds. Such pension funds have historically been major backers of the industry, and some are highly influential and diversified players with significant private markets allocations.

Historically, it has been more difficult for defined *contribution* (and self-invested) pensions to commit to traditional LP funds because of the need for daily pricing and liquidity for DC pensions. One notable exception is the Australian Superannuation scheme, which is an exceptionally well-funded system and which pools vast sums of capital, giving the managers much more flexibility and freedom to invest in illiquid assets than most other types of corporate contribution schemes. However, as political pressure to give pensioners better access to private markets increases, the market is responding with new vehicle types that can better accommodate defined contribution schemes too (see Chapter 9).

Cultures of Commitment

Investor preferences are also likely to be influenced by cultural context and familiarity with private markets differs vastly between countries.

France, for instance, has a long history of high-net-worth individuals investing directly into private markets funds. There are strong cultural, structural and regulatory factors behind this, including specialised funds designed for retail and high-net-worth participation, often with favourable tax treatment. France is home to a vibrant mid-market private equity sector, and to an extent, HNWs have made up for a relatively limited source of domestic institutional capital. There is also a network of French banks, wealth managers and advisers to distribute the products, and as a result, wealthy French people have a long tradition of investing substantial proportions of their wealth in illiquid products.

Italy is also fairly advanced in private markets participation among individuals, despite a relatively small domestic private capital scene. Like France, it has tax-advantage vehicles encouraging long-term investment and a decent private bank distribution network. Switzerland also has a tradition of wealth investment into private markets, with a qualified investor regime and a respected network of private banks.

Despite recent rule changes in the United States and the United Kingdom to try to encourage more individual participation in private markets, these jurisdictions are relative laggards – highlighting the importance of culture, behaviours and market structures – it's not just about regulation. One way they may catch up is through the adoption of digital investment platforms, where accredited individuals can take a slice of top-tier funds with not much more than a few clicks. The minimums can be as low as €50k, and much of the administrative hassle is optimised and online.

Unlisted, Closed-ended. . . Retail Friendly?

The above subtitle seems paradoxical, but there are various regimes that have long encouraged retail participation in traditional private markets – often with tax incentives.

AU Australia: Early Stage Venture Capital Limited Partnerships (ESVCLPs)

- Partnership vehicles investing in early-stage, high-growth companies.
- Investors get a 10% non-refundable tax offset on new investments, and profits on eligible investments are tax-free.
- Managed like VC funds but with government certification.

FR France – Fonds Communs de Placement dans l'Innovation (FCPI) & Fonds d'Investissement de Proximité (FIP)

- Mutual fund-like structures for innovative SMEs (FCPI) or regional businesses (FIP).
- Tax perks: up to 18% income tax credit (recently reduced from 25%), and gains tax-free if held for at least five years.

IT Italy – PIR (Piani Individuali di Risparmio)

- Not a fund type per se, but a tax wrapper around funds that invest in Italian SMEs.
- Tax perks: No capital gains tax if held for at least five years.

(see also 'The Tax Trap', page 115)

For some, there will be no substitution for the direct cash flow of making real fund commitments, and it is worth the long commitment and operational complexity. But for those seeking lower entry minimums, less commitment and/or greater liquidity, read on. . . .

9

Gated Evergreens

'Be discreet in all things and so render it unnecessary to be mysterious about any'.

– **Duke of Wellington**

For those that can scrape together a few hundred thousand dollars in investable assets, there has been an explosion of interest in a type of open-ended unlisted 'evergreen' vehicle that gives investors direct exposure to private markets assets without the complexity and high ticket sizes of direct investments into funds.

Such vehicles are currently referred to as 'semi-liquid evergreens' but this is not a good description – so before we go further, we need to identify some better terminology. A more accurate label for such vehicles might be 'open-ended evergreens' with conditional liquidity – the fund manager turns the liquidity on and off, or to mix metaphors, to gate entry and exit. So I will refer to them as 'gated evergreens'. This has the added advantage of sounding like an exclusive housing estate: *Gated Evergreens*.

In any case, there has been a surge of offerings in the market, across all the major strategies and multi-strategies.

Pros and Unknowns of Gated Evergreens

Most gated evergreens co-invest in deals as they come through a manager's pipeline. This means the funds can only be offered – and grow – at a rate that correlates with the opportunities coming through the managers' deal funnel. The bigger the manager, the faster they can scale up. Some private markets strategies are more conducive to this churn than others – private credit, for instance, can be quickly put to work. Primary private equity investments are much slower, and so there needs to be a deal machine of significant size flowing through opportunities for the evergreen to soak up. For third-party multi-strategy funds with access to the opportunities of third-party managers, this will be easier.

So for private markets managers themselves, the attractions are clear: they can continuously rake in capital (subject to the deal flow constraints just mentioned), and so grow their assets-under-management continuously, and their fee income, so long as they can source sufficient deal flow.

For investors, there are numerous attractions. For one, gated evergreen vehicles are 'fully funded' from day one (pre-loaded with live investments, not just blind pool commitments). This is a big advantage versus traditional closed-endeds because it means they offer immediate exposure to private markets – there is no delay between commitment and investment (the so-called J-curve). This can mean the performance of such evergreens can, in theory at least, be superior to that of traditional LP funds. This fact is even attracting institutional investors who are quite capable of investing directly into traditional LP funds.

Another big draw is the simplicity. Not only do gated evergreens cut out the hassle of fund selection (as a traditional fund-of-funds would also do), but they also simplify the management of cash flows and reinvestment. And yet, you still have direct exposure to the underlying assets. These vehicles aren't proxies for private markets – they are the real thing. The complexities are still there – it's just that, unlike with a traditional closed-ended funds, they sit with the manager, not the investor.

To make the whole thing work, the manager has to be very careful about the liquidity profile of the underlying assets. The fund will often 'advertise' a sub-asset-class as its main focus, say private equity or private credit or private real estate, but this will always be part of a broader asset mix. Private credit tends to be a very prominent part of multi-asset funds (often significantly more than half), given that its shorter duration and large addressable market are helpful in managing liquidity and putting money to work; there tends to be a relatively little exposure to primary private equity and real asset funds, given their much less liquid profile. In addition, there will usually be an allocation to secondaries funds, which are also shorter duration and provide immediate access to underlying assets.

On top of this, the vehicles also need a portion in cash or cash equivalents to lubricate redemption requests (known as the 'liquidity sleeve'). While the presence of cash in the vehicle will be dilutive of returns, this is no different to the situation for LPs who must keep their committed capital on standby.

The Main Types of Gated Evergreens

As open-ended vehicles, investors buy into at the prevailing book value of the underlying assets – but their ability to sell is subject to constraints. These constraints differ slightly depending on the specific type of vehicle.

These vehicles have many attractions, but they are only 'semi-liquid' *most of the time*. Some of the time (and it's when you want it most), they are entirely illiquid, since selling your share is at the managers' discretion.

In the United States, there are three main types: 'Interval funds' are, at present, the largest segment. These vehicles allow investors to buy in at any time, at the net asset value of the underlying assets, but they restrict redemptions to certain set intervals, usually quarterly (this is the semi-liquid aspect). At each interval, the investor can usually only sell a portion of their holdings, often no more than a quarter. These repurchases are also done at fair value or 'NAV'.

Similar to these are 'tender offer vehicles', which are also evergreen, open-ended, NAV-based and semi-liquid, but with a few differences: the redemptions are not regular but at the manager's discretion and they are done via tenders, where investors submit requests that may be accepted in full, in part, or rejected. Because they are less liquid than interval funds, these are only open to accredited (sophisticated) investors, not to just anyone.

Also for US investors, unlisted Business Development Companies, encountered in Chapter 8, are popular options. These are particularly well suited to private credit strategies. They typically offer quarterly windows during which investors can sell, but this right can be suspended by the manager.

Meanwhile, European Long-Term Investment Funds or ELTIFs were introduced back in 2016 by the EU to encourage individual investment in long-term illiquid asset classes. Their uptake has been significantly slower – the total market is only about €15bn at the time of writing, but the features are worthy of the most committed barbarian. Minimum holding periods of five years, or even eight years, are common, with redemptions requiring a long notice period (90–180 days) and available on an annual or semi-annual basis.

In the United Kingdom, LTAFs – Long-Term Asset Funds – are increasingly popular among trustees of defined contribution schemes and master trusts as a way of entering private markets. They have also been given the nod by the regulator, so they could be set to become the vehicle-of-choice for individual investors looking to make commitments to private markets via their self-invested pensions or savings plans.

Provenance of Gated Evergreens

So-called 'semi-liquid evergreens' were invented by a Swiss private markets manager called Partners Group back in 2001 to allow smaller institutions and wealthy individuals to access private markets. The structure was a Luxembourg-based SICAV, effectively an offshore version of these vehicles, with the same fundamental features as those above. For a long time, Partners Group was the only major player in the market, and everyone else simply looked on – but recently their popularity has soared as ever more investors seek to escape the public markets but retain the ease and user-experience of mutual funds and ETFs. Between 2022 and 2024, assets managed by evergreens grew from $200 to nearly $350bn, according to Morningstar. PitchBook reckons the market will be at $1trn within five years.[1]

At the time of writing, such funds can't be bought on most online platforms, but only through a financial adviser. The rules and vehicles in each jurisdiction differ in terms of who is able to invest, the minimum investment thresholds and the amount of leverage a fund is allowed.

Thanks to Partners Group, there is some time-tested data to give the rest of the market confidence. But since Partners was going it alone for so long, it's not the most diverse dataset. The Swiss are masters of precision instruments, but we can't yet be certain that the gated evergreen is a demonstrably anti-fragile structure as it rolls out across the wider investment market. There is certainly a significant element of judgement and diligence required.

However, the structure has already had its first big test – and it passed. In late 2022 and 2023, investors in Blackstone's unlisted real estate income trust (BREIT) faced a potential liquidity crunch.

Barbarians Close the Gates

Coming out of the Covid-inspired lockdowns, interest rates were rising, tech was booming but confidence in the real world – such as buildings and atoms – was waning. The wider real estate investment trust market was tumbling, but the value of Blackstone's vehicle was holding up relatively well. Some investors, notably those from Asia who were facing the double punishment of a rising dollar, saw the opportunity to cash-out of BREIT at higher valuations than the wider market. This caused a spike in redemption requests that put the model to the test.

The BREIT vehicle allowed investors to redeem up to 2% of their holdings per month and 5% per quarter. But as redemption requests grew, Blackstone enforced its contractual mechanism to gate access to leave the fund, restricting outflows. By late 2023, the outflow pressure eased, confidence grew and the fund maintained its income distribution.

This is precisely how you would want a manager to behave under such circumstances. The last thing a true barbarian wants is for a manager to cave to the emotions of plastic barbarians and fire-sell assets. In fact, Blackstone went further. It proactively communicated with investors to emphasise the strong rationale for the vehicle's outperformance relative to the rest of the sector. And it secured a $4bn strategic investment from the University of California, a commitment that it back-stopped with Blackstone's balance sheet to the tune of $1bn and a guarantee to UC of an 11.25% return over six years. These sent strong signals of confidence to the market and quickly scotched what could otherwise have been a longer running drama.

Some point to the episode as an example of the shortcomings and risks of the model. To me, it looks like a vehicle – and a manager – behaving as they were supposed to. If anything, Blackstone went slightly overboard in appeasement.

Breaking into a Multi-trillion Market

One reason fund managers are so excited about unlisted evergreens is that they could be the key to unlocking pensions. The old-style defined benefit schemes were big investors in traditional closed-end funds, but modern defined contribution schemes require daily pricing and liquidity. This has deterred many trustees from committing to private markets. It's not that such schemes are prevented from such investment currently, but the pensions market is heavily guided by convention and – in the United States – litigation, where cases are frequently brought against trustees for investing in 'expensive' and complex asset classes.

But a combination of market innovations and (more importantly) shifting political guidance is encouraging adoption of unlisted evergreens. Private markets managers are also lobbying hard to get political endorsement – and succeeding. They have argued that it isn't fair that ordinary pensioners are missing out on the performance and diversification benefits of private markets. In the United States, for instance, there are $12 trillion of assets owned by 12 million '401k' pensioners. And there are increasing signals that politicians will give the managers of that capital the 'cover' to invest in such assets. There are even hopes that private markets will become a small exposure within 'Target Date funds', which are default components of most DC schemes, giving pensioners automatic exposure to private markets. Meanwhile, in the United Kingdom, the Mansion House Compact gives similar political cover to DC trustees to invest in private markets.

It's bizarre to think that the investment assets with the longest time-horizon in any individual's portfolio – their pension – has struggled to invest in an attractive asset-class because the underlying assets are somewhat illiquid. Technicalities aside, pensions and private markets are a very natural fit.

For individual investors, the implications of this, are: if you have a DC scheme, greater private markets exposure or optionality may be coming your way. If you are looking to invest independently, there may be a wave of demand for unlisted evergreens on the way. This will not directly push up prices – valuation is determined by the fundamentals of the underlying assets. But it could make *access* to funds somewhat constrained over time.

Trust and Track Record

There are broadly two types of firms offering gated evergreens (and they are pretty much all marketed as 'semi-liquid' vehicles).

There are asset managers that offer deep access across a diversified pool of private markets funds. And there are private markets specialists, which offer more concentrated exposure, often with more exposure to direct investment, through BDCs, REITs and investment-trust like vehicles. For now, the providers of such vehicles remain relatively concentrated. For instance, Blackstone started offering products to wealthy individuals two decades ago. In 2024, it saw $23bn of inflows into its evergreen products, accounting for 20% of the market. However, things are evolving rapidly, with established private markets managers launching new evergreen products regularly.

The diversification benefits of multi-asset strategies are worth emphasising. Nothing is good all the time, and there is no point trying to predict what will be good next when you are committing your capital for long periods. At the time of writing, the performance data from Morningstar and PitchBook showed a 7.6% median return from all private markets evergreens in the year to the end of April 2025. Secondaries were the best performing, credit was faring well, while private equity was in the doldrums, and real estate was positively depressed.

Things you might consider when selecting a vehicle are the alignment that the asset allocator, fund selector or private markets manager has with the performance of the vehicle itself. Are there embedded conflicts, such as being merely incentivised by inflow volume or (unrealised) NAV growth, or do they have real skin in the game, for instance, by having fees related to realised gains. And also ensure there is a proper waterfall arrangement, whereby the classic carried interest hurdle is properly observed.

Seek clarity on how the manager would behave in a crisis and, indeed, how they behave generally. What is the historic fulfilment ratio for redemptions and how often have the barbarians shut the gates? If there is volatility, perhaps there are liquidity management challenges.

Some funds actually charge early redemption fees – say, if you choose to exit inside of five years, for instance. There are some signs the market is moving away from this.[2]

Another angle might be to look at inflows by type of investor. With no offence to individuals, but if 95% of the investors are retail and there is very little institutional involvement, this could be a signal that the wider market does not rate the manager. Or there could be a good reason for it. If liquidity really does matter to you, you might want a fund with a diverse investor base, so they don't all try to rush out when, for instance currency markets move in one direction.

You should also look at the source of deal flow and their access to opportunities across not only primary investments but also co-invest, secondaries and any sub-asset classes you may be interested in. Is the manager pumping the evergreen full of 'ageing' deals that they can't otherwise off-load? That might not be a great sign.

What is their mechanism for keeping things fair from a value perspective as investors come in and out of the fund (so existing investors aren't diluted or new investors aren't overpaying). This is referred to as equalisation and it is normally handled by 'series accounting' whereby inflows and outflows are batched into 'series' and their performance (and therefore fees payable) are calculated accordingly. You might also look at their NAV construction itself. How conservative are their discounting methods when valuing assets? If historic valuations diverge from listed equivalents, find out why. There may be a good reason, as with the BREIT episode above.

For investors with anything between several thousand and a few million dollars to invest in private markets, gated evergreens are a way to invest like a true barbarian, with direct exposure to the performance of a diversified pool of private assets. It's still early days for this market – evergreens account for little more than 1% of the total assets under management in private markets at the time of writing – but at the very least, it's 'one to watch'.

Gated Evergreens – Fund Selection Checklist

1. Do you want single strategy/single manager exposure or diversified and independent management?
2. If you are investing in a diversified pool of funds and managers, are the underlying managers a 'brand name'?
3. Is the fund accessible to you? Check eligibility requirements.
4. Does the manager have 'skin in the game'? Check incentives and alignment structures.
5. What is the approach to liquidity and redemptions in normal times, and in extremis?

6. What is the mix of the existing investor base, by type (institutional, retail, etc)?
7. What are the fund sources of deal flow?
8. How does the fund value assets?
9. What is its past performance?
10. Am I comfortable committing long-term capital?

For insight into gated evergreen, scan this QR code.

10

Listed Private Capital

> *'By blending the vigour of his barbarian heritage with the refined institutions of Rome, Clovis secured the loyalty of his Gallo-Roman subjects and extended his dominion. . .'*
>
> **– Edward Gibbon**

One of the simplest ways for the aspiring barbarian to get private markets exposure is through the stock markets. Let's be clear. Just because it is simple does not make it inferior. And just because it is 'public' markets does not make it a contradiction. The 'private' in private markets refers to the way the underlying assets are held. The strategic barbarian exploits any and all means to gain effective access to the performance of such assets.

I will go further. I consider many listed private capital structures as offering the best-of-both worlds – public and private – in a way that makes perfect sense for investors of any type, and particularly for individuals. It has all the advantages of stock market investing: it's familiar, straightforward, you get immediate exposure, and you can buy and sell quickly and cheaply. And it has the additional benefit that you are effectively piggybacking off the strong governance structures and aligned incentives of the underlying funds, giving you instant, diverse exposure to the rough and tumble of the productive economy.

As far as I can tell, there is only really one wrinkle, and it's not something that keeps me awake at night: it is difficult for fund managers to use these vehicles to accumulate ever more capital for themselves.

Broadly, there are two types of listed private capital companies. Listed private capital funds and listed private capital managers. There are also a few companies that combine both.

Listed Private Capital Funds

These companies are effectively listed closed-end fund investors – they invest the public company's balance sheet capital into fixed-life closed-ended private markets funds or directly into private assets (i.e. they are the fund itself).

For historic and regulatory reasons, there are slightly different approaches between jurisdictions.

US Business Development Companies

In the United States, BDCs were created in the mid-20th century for stock market investors to get access to private companies, usually in middle-market debt, and sometimes equity. These companies must invest 70% of their capital into such opportunities and distribute 90% of their income to shareholders in order to avoid corporation tax.

This is very similar to being a closed-end LP, without all the costs and hassle. The downside is the regulatory restrictions on the manager mentioned above, constraining agility.

The market for BDCs was slow to pick up, until the modern private markets industry got going this century.

Just prior to the GFC, the biggest barbarian fund managers were scratching their heads, trying to figure out how to tap into the public market investor. The big attraction, from their perspective, was not only new sources of capital, but the fact that such capital is perpetual – unlike closed-end funds, which have to be constantly wound down and raised afresh.

The first major attempt was in 2004 when Apollo raised $1bn BDC. Such are the vagaries of the private markets that, while Apollo's flotation was successful, it was not appreciated by the market. The fees looked too high, the investments too esoteric. As it turned out, public markets were not wrong to be sceptical. Apollo's BDC invested in the dying days of a pre-GFC bull market, and so the vehicle underperformed for an extended period. This soured the approach in the minds of investors and barbarians alike. And yet, the vehicle itself is remarkably suitable for the burgeoning private credit market. Had timings and events been different, BDCs could have emerged much sooner as a major conduit.

But eventually memories fade or animal spirits re-emerge, and so BDCs have enjoyed a major renaissance. Their assets under management have risen from $127bn in assets in 2020 to $438bn by the end of 2024, a compound annual growth rate of 28%. About half of this has been fuelled by the establishment of non-listed BDCs targeting wealthy investors.

Prominent examples are Blackstone Private Credit, worth about $60bn, and Ares Capital Corporation, the largest public BDC with $25bn in assets in 2025.

EU and UK Investment Companies

In Europe, there is a small but well-established population of listed private capital funds that trace their roots back to the earliest joint-stock companies, such as the Dutch and British East India companies. These vehicles began as temporary but eventually became evergreen trading companies and became known as 'investment trusts' in the United Kingdom or 'investment companies' in Continental Europe.

The first modern investment trusts were set up around the turn of the 20th century, and they helped finance and build the major infrastructure projects of their day: the US railroads were built with the capital of British (particularly Scottish) individuals and families. But they fell from favour, as stock market investors began to prefer the transparency and governance of operating companies that made profits directly rather than passing them through. Most of those that survived turned away from private infrastructure projects and instead invested in other listed companies. But several have become modern barbarians, investing in private markets funds. Some are 'single manager' LPs, so they tend to only invest in the funds of one manager. An example in the UK is Hg Capital Trust, which only invests in the funds of Hg, a software-focused private equity firm. Others are more like LP funds of funds, investing in a wider pool of LP funds and also exercising various 'guerrilla-style real options', as outlined in Chapter 5.

The Discount Code

You might be wondering why I said these funds are good for investors, but that fund managers are less keen.

This is to do with a feature of listed funds, which is often presented as a bug – the ability for the share price to disconnect from the value of the underlying portfolio.

Like all public companies, the share price of listed private capital funds is a function of the demand for their shares. When a new investor buys into the company, the share price might go up, but it has no effect at all on the value of the underlying assets. When you think of it, this is no different from any listed company – if the shares of a listed manufacturing company rise, their accountants don't mark up the value of their real estate or machinery in accordance. In effect, all ordinary listed operating companies are closed ended – they don't have to buy more inventory every time someone buys their shares.

The reason it seems odd to people in the public funds world is merely in relation to mutual funds and other open-ended listed funds, which must buy or sell underlying holdings every time investors want to buy or sell their own fund units. This works fine if the mutual fund is just buying highly liquid stocks like anyone can. But it doesn't work for the slow, patient, private markets model, where the fund manager needs freedom and time to make the right decisions. By being closed ended, these funds are not forced to buy or sell anything – their shares trade with reference to, but independently from, the underlying assets. This makes them a fantastic vehicle for owning 'illiquid' private assets through a public market vehicle. The underlying assets are kept separate, and their governance is kept pristine.

So what's the problem?

Well, it means that the share price of these funds will either trade at a premium or a discount to the 'net asset value' of the underlying assets. Historically, most such companies have traded at a significant and persistent discount. This is true for BDCs, and it is particularly true for European investment funds. And when you trade at a discount to 'NAV', it is very difficult to raise new money through secondary offerings. The manager just has a fixed amount of capital that it can grow, distribute (especially in the case of BDCs) or retain. And that has been a source of frustration in a private markets industry that is growing so quickly in so many other ways.

I suspect much of the impetus behind gated evergreens in the previous chapter comes from this constraint.

The Correlation 'Problem'

For institutional investors and intermediaries, one of the attractions of private markets is diversification – in a narrow sense. And if you are getting your exposure to it through public markets, it defeats the purpose, because you are fully exposed to stock market volatility. But I don't think most individual investors care about 'volatility' or short-term correlations. They care about returns. Certainly, those with a genuinely barbaric mindset couldn't care less. In fact, volatility will be an opportunity to 'buy the dips' at fleetingly large discounts – a massive advantage that individuals have over bureaucratic institutional decision-making. So from the perspective of the average Joe investor, I wouldn't consider any of this to be a downside.

One extreme example of such an opportunity occurred during the Global Financial Crisis, when the share prices of many listed private capital companies tanked. Some listed funds traded at discounts to NAV in excess of 90% – what analysts call 'capitulation levels'. But those (technically uncommitted) barbarian stockholders that remained patient, just watched as the market gradually changed from a voting machine to a weighing machine. Meanwhile, a bold few continued to fill their boots.

The purist might argue that such stocks are not private markets proper, because the shares are not formally tied to the value of the assets; they are a function of supply and demand of the shares, and that is all. But over time, there will be an extremely strong correlation between the two, so for the patient investor, these vehicles are a very good, simple option for getting high quality or diversified exposure to private markets, with a very low cost of entry – let's say $100 on the online platform of your choice.

You might wonder why on earth such funds trade at a discount – if they provide such access to sought-after private markets funds. Various technical explanations have been put forward, but none are convincing. I don't have a good answer for you – other than maybe public markets intermediaries just don't 'get' private markets. Analysts who cover such listed private capital funds tend to focus not on the overall share price performance but on how closely the price tracks the underlying value. If it trades above, then it is a premium, and so they tend to say *it's expensive*. If it trades below, it is at a discount, and so this must signal there is something dodgy about it. This might sound like a caricature. If only. This means they are overlooked, there isn't huge liquidity in most of their stocks (relative to other public companies, that is), and they are, hence, the best kept secret on the stock markets. The individual barbarian investor can buy high-quality managers and diversified pools of funds at heavy discounts – more cheaply than are available to institutions that would buy the actual LP interests directly! And the only reasons I can see that the big LPs don't go this route are a mixture of bureaucratic constraints and their need to put to work enormous sums of capital that could move the market in relatively small, *relatively* illiquid listed stocks.

If their popularity never improves, and so the discount is maintained, you will still benefit from the same upward trajectory of the share price as the underlying assets. Unless you bought in at the IPO in 1989 or 1899 or whenever, then you really have nothing to complain about. And even then. There is a phrase in listed private equity: *you can't eat the NAV* – so just focus on the share price.

It might seem incredible that the public markets can undervalue such assets so systemically. But even in so-called efficient markets, value is subjective and in the eye of the beholder. Given that individuals have such a weak voice, stock market gatekeepers call the shots, and why would they care about shareholder returns? Their priorities, very clearly, are liquidity, price discovery and public disclosure. Anything that does not tick most of those boxes is de-rated in their estimation. When confronted with such priorities, the true barbarian wards off evil.

Back in 2011, I was involved in raising awareness of the logic of such listed funds. But the analyst community was more interested in Neil Woodford. He was the UK's most famous 'star fund manager' and he made his name buying big tobacco and shunning tech during the dot-com bubble. They also liked him because he didn't manage some fuddy-duddy old investment trust; he managed a highly scalable open-ended investment company. These work the opposite way to investment trusts – they swell and shrink their capital base according to the demand for their units. Expanding beyond listed companies, Woodford decided to try his hand at a bit of venture capital along with his income-generating public stocks that were on the fund label. It was a classic liquidity mismatch. When listing rules put him 'over-weight' on the private portion of his underlying assets, his investments underperformed, and his investors lost confidence, but he couldn't sell the underlying private assets. He was committed, but his investors weren't (or didn't think they were). The fund was gated and ultimately wound down. His investors lost £1bn and had to wait years to get their capital back.

The Tax Trap

The provision of capital to start-ups or underserved smaller companies can be a political 'issue'. That's why you will find tax-advantaged private capital structures in various regions. But such perks always come with strings attached that can often undermine the investment proposition.

In the United States, BDC rules are not ideal for equity funding, but the market has adapted, and so they have become a powerful private lending vehicle.

In the United Kingdom, Venture Capital Trusts offer very juicy tax incentives: buy in at the initial offering, hold shares for five years and pay no tax on dividends or capital gains. (South Africa has a similar regime.) But they can only invest in companies that have less than seven years of trading history – just one of many rules that bind the freedom of managers and entrepreneurs – and remember, agility is a key performance driver in private markets. VCTs must also be listed on London's main market, and these (usually quite small) vehicles are therefore exposed to the huge compliance and reporting burden of the largest listed companies – a fact that, ironically enough, creates an equity gap for small and new VCT managers.

As a rule of thumb: exploit tax perks where they align with good investments – but never let a tax break be the main justification.

Listed Private Capital Managers

The other main type of listed private capital company is a listed manager – effectively a listed GP. These are the biggest private capital stocks there are – the Blackstones, KKRs, EQTs and Apollos, to name but a few.

The stock market remains a good home for large, well-diversified businesses that have a clear path to continued profitability. Such has been the success of private markets that this now applies to many of the larger fund managers.

When you invest in such a manager's stock, you are not just investing *like* a barbarian, you are actually becoming one. You benefit from both the fee streams of the funds that are managed (such as the fund management fees and the monitoring fees charged to portfolio companies) and you are also a beneficiary of the success of the funds they manage, through a share of their carried interest and manager co-investment in their funds.

We will see in Chapter 11 that there is a potential misalignment of incentives between investors and managers around fund size – since the manager earns much more in absolute terms for larger funds. From this, you can see that when you invest in a listed manager, your incentives realign with the Masters of Universe themselves, the frontline barbarians. It's arguably a closer alignment than if you were a big institution investing as an LP. By the same logic, such managers may be encouraged to raise funds for various strategies just to increase their assets under management, rather than because there is a compelling market opportunity in, say, corporate sub-prime real estate. But as an owner of the manager itself, what is good for them is good for you.

The First Listed Mega Manager

While listed private capital managers have long been a feature of European stock markets (see 'Europe's idiosyncratic listed managers') the listing of mainstream private capital giants in the United States is a fairly recent phenomenon.

Blackstone was the first mega manager to go public, back in 2007. It was the biggest IPO in the United States for years and since nobody had done anything like it and certainly not at that scale before, setting the IPO price was very much a finger in the air activity. As natural born dealmakers, the founders did not underplay their hand.

In stock markets, timing is everything. Blackstone went public at the top of the market, on the eve of the Global Financial Crisis, at $31 a share. You might think buying into a leveraged buyout shop in the summer of 2007 would have ended up as a very fateful move. But those who didn't panic during the crisis and hung on did not regret it. Eighteen years later, it is up nearly 500% at a market cap of around $180bn.

Blackstone's own governance journey is a neat microcosm and telling of public/private trade-offs. Initially, its CEO and modern day Clovis, Stephen Schwarzman, was ambivalent about listing and only did so on condition that shareholders were disempowered. He did not want to give them the ability to nominate or depose directors. So Blackstone's clever lawyers borrowed the master limited partnership model, until then only really used by the oil and gas industry.

As a result, the original public investors in Blackstone were not technically shareholders, they were LPs. But this structure meant it wasn't eligible for inclusion in the S&P 500 and so would not be covered by passive index trackers. So in 2019, the company shifted its structure to a C-Corporation, sacrificing some management control on the altar of liquidity.

GP Stakes

Back over in the private-private capital market, there is a growing awareness of the value buried in private fund management companies – even ones that are much smaller than the mega US managers – hence there is a booming private market for acquiring stakes in GP fund managers. At the time of writing in mid-2025, the market for new public issues has been moribund, but I suspect, when the IPO markets pick up, we will see many more private markets managers going public to provide an exit to these GP-stake investors. We may also start to see the first listings of big venture capital managers, which will introduce a very interesting dynamic into public markets.

Europe's Idiosyncratic Listed Managers

In Europe, there is a diverse population of listed private capital companies, and some have been around for a very long time. But their provenance is highly idiosyncratic. A few examples:

Eurazeo is France's oldest listed private equity company. It was founded in 1881 as 'Gaz et Eau' to invest in French utilities, deeply embedded into the French business elite. Around the millennium, it transformed from an industrial conglomerate into a private equity player that is structurally comparable to Blackstone (but much smaller) and it also provides direct exposure to its funds.

In the United Kingdom, 3i was originally set up by the UK government in 1945 to rebuild Britain's war-ravaged economy and pump money into small private enterprises. At one time, there was, proverbially at least, a local 3i office on every major high street in Britain. It was privatised in the 1990s, floated on the stock market and transformed itself into a modern listed private equity and infrastructure manager and fund.

In Scandinavia, one of the wealthiest families of industrialists, the Wallenbergs, own Sweden's oldest bank, SEB, and have controlling stakes in some of the biggest companies, from Ericsson and Saab to AstraZeneca and Electrolux. They set up a private equity arm in the 1990s called EQT, to diversify its portfolio out of large listed industrial companies. EQT itself was listed on Nasdaq Stockholm in 2019 and has more than €200bn in assets under management. The Wallenberg's main listed holding company, Investor AB, retains a significant stake in EQT.

There are an ever-growing number of ways for the individual barbarian to access private markets outperformance via the stock market. According to LPX, the size of the total listed private markets sector has grown from about €50bn in 2010 to more than €650bn in 2024. At the same time, the size of the public markets has remained static and have become ever more concentrated. It's like a colossal, slow-motion reverse takeover of the public markets itself.

Or is it the other way around?

For insight into specific listed private equity companies, scan this QR code.

11

Lost in Liquidity

'We have it beaten into our heads that public is safe and private is risky... But what if we're wrong? What if private is both safe and risky, and public is both safe and risky?'

— **Marc Rowan, Apollo**

You've been very patient (and that's a good sign) but by now you probably just want to know what to expect from investing in private markets — the return, the risk, and whether, on balance, the whole thing is worth it. We will come to this shortly. But first, we need to deal with something else: liquidity.

Most people coming to private markets for the first time will already be familiar with stock market investment. But experiences of the stock market — and the standard 'techniques that are used to build liquid investment portfolios — come with a whole host of assumptions that just don't apply to private markets funds. This is mainly because the underlying privately held assets are highly 'illiquid' — they cannot be bought and sold quickly and cheaply.

An investor in a closed-ended private markets fund *can* usually sell out of their position, but it is costly and they are better off assuming that all investment decisions are effectively irreversible. Shares in a listed company are like a bubbling brook — always trading up and down. A commitment to a private markets fund is like a big, solid block of ice. It will thaw into returns eventually, but you aren't in charge of when.

This illiquidity creates genuine complexity and is a perpetual source of confusion among commentators who are more familiar with stock markets. So we must look at just why private markets are such a fish out of water in a world of liquidity.

The Liquidity Delusion

The simple solution to dealing with illiquidity is simply to be patient. Unfortunately, in today's hyperactive world, even for big institutional investors with very long-time horizons, this is not realistic. Therefore, techniques that make the investor's position easier to sell and trade than the underlying assets themselves have become very popular.

But there is always a price to pay, somewhere.

Perhaps that is why illiquidity is invariably expressed as an irredeemable flaw, making the asset-class unsuitable for any except the most eccentric or reckless investor. It's a perspective that reminds me of Huxley's *A Brave New World*, where promiscuity is socially praised and encouraged, while commitment and restraint are shameful. Private markets certainly go against the zeitgeist. They jar with the dopamine-addicted, attention-deficit hyperactivity disorder of our age. In a world of fast food, high-frequency-trading, 24-hour-news cycles. . . private markets are slow. They require a different cadence and a different mindset.

One of the fallacies of modern behavioural economics is that maximising choice is a rational and optimal approach to fulfilling needs and desires. But every civilised person voluntarily constrains their behaviour to an astonishing degree. It manifests as self-discipline and those with it prosper. In today's secular society, a rational economist might consider marriage to be redundant. But those with the most freedom (the wealthy) are most likely to form such commitments. Mankind's potential is only ever realised through limitation.

It is the same with investment. If you want to do great things and survive the adventure, you need to bind yourself to the mast, like Odysseus. The sirens will call on all sides to distract you, but hyperactivity is the enemy of good investment. Private markets are a systematised constraint. Through such voluntary limitation, investors give private equity fund managers a corresponding amount of freedom. Financial theorists, who see no link between how they live their own lives and economics, have watched this bizarre and asymmetric marriage of private markets manager and investor with bemusement. And they have rationalised it away through the creation of a causal fallacy: the illiquidity premium.

It goes like this: investors in private equity funds should be rewarded for giving up their freedoms with a higher return. And according to modern portfolio theory, you only get higher returns by taking on more risk. By continually providing high returns, therefore, private equity is ipso facto a high-risk activity.

But managers of illiquid assets don't provide higher returns *in recompense* for limiting your options. They provide higher returns *because* they limit your options, and you provide them with latitude. This means illiquid funds don't need to take on more risk to reward your commitment. The commitment itself is the source of the reward.

Liquidity is like an escape hatch on a submarine. You can use it when you are underwater, but it's not advisable. Once you're above the surface, liquidity no longer matters. You'll be getting out anyway.

The cost of keeping your options open is very high. One of the pioneer investors in private markets, David Swenson, manager of Yale's endowment, actively avoided liquid investments – for a long-term oriented investor, the cost was too high. In the 36 years he managed the endowment, until his death in 2021, he grew the fund from $1 to $36bn, with an unprecedented and large allocation to private markets.

You don't have to stand back very far to see how bizarre this liquidity obsession has become, and how odd it is to want to protect ordinary investors from committed forms of investment. People buy property all the time (usually their home). This is an exceedingly illiquid asset, made even more so by most tax regimes. And most politicians like the idea of people owning their own homes. Meanwhile, you can buy a ten-year fixed term bond on the internet in five minutes, with no declaration of sophistication. The only odd thing about private equity's illiquidity is by contrast with the hyper liquidity of public markets.

To adapt Mark Rowan's quote at the top of this chapter, private markets are illiquid and that can be a good and a bad thing. Public markets are liquid and that can be a good and a bad thing.

The Panic Premium

The second thing you'll hear about private equity at business school is the backhanded compliment that it smooths the volatility of investment portfolios. Then in the next breath, the lecturer will add, but it isn't *really* less volatile, it just masks volatility because private equity valuations are 'stale' – they aren't constantly traded, so they are out-of-date and, particularly at times of market panic, they are not marked down fast or hard enough.

Again, it's a description of private equity from the perspective of constantly traded stock market investments, and it is therefore nonsense.

A listed company is like a dinghy floating on an ocean of market sentiment. Because the company can be bought and sold at any moment, its valuation rises and falls constantly on the waves of sentiment.

A private equity backed company is like a dinghy sailing down a smooth sea lane, protected on all sides by a giant floating rig, which is the private equity fund structure. There are no waves of market sentiment buffeting this dinghy because the private equity firm controls its ownership.

While private equity backed companies are always held with the intention to sell, private equity owners are in control of when they sell. They are never forced into it and not a single share can be sold without their permission.

So does it make sense for a private equity manager to try to constantly revalue their companies based on what that asset would fetch in the open market? Well, does an asset have an intrinsic value that is divorced from the value its owner would be willing to sell it for? Would such a value be 'fair'?

Private equity valuations don't smooth over volatility. They are inherently less volatile. Public markets create volatility. They are inherently more volatile. That's really all that can be said about it.

One logical approach for private equity firms would be to just hold their investments 'at-cost' – the price they bought the assets for. And then they'd mark them up (or down) when the asset is sold. This was never going to work as the industry grew, because the volatility in the rest of the investors' portfolios kept making their relative exposure to private markets look erratic.

So these days, private equity managers value their assets much more regularly. They look at comparables and perform various rites and then send their LPs the resulting quarterly valuation updates. These aren't market prices, they are called 'fair' valuations – what the manager believes two independent parties might agree upon in an orderly transaction. The fact that such fair values are not the automatic settlement price derived from unconstrained trading does make them stale or arbitrary or somehow less accurate. They are values assigned by careful and considered owners who are not obligated to sell (or buy) continually.

A telling indication that you can't just assign a liquid value to an illiquid asset is the fact that private equity owned companies are usually sold at a mark-up to their latest valuation, or they see an uplift just prior to sale. A cynic might say this is because private equity managers are systematically undervaluing their companies but it's actually because private equity managers are in control of when, where and how they sell a company. In that context, one would expect the seller to achieve a strategic premium over the 'fair' market value. Otherwise, why would they sell?

For instance, at the time of writing in mid-2025, the past five months have seen the S&P 500 fall nearly 20% and then bounce back to almost exactly where it was. During that time, very few private equity firms chose to sell their companies. Remember, public market liquidity is like an escape hatch on a submarine. You can open it when you are underwater, but do you really want that option? Private equity doesn't give it.

Charlie Munger has said he believes pension fund managers like private equity because they don't have to mark down the valuation of their portfolios as much as they should in the middle of panics. But does it really make sense to say that the value of comparable private equity owned companies really fell 20% during those months and then bounced back? I think a more interesting question is, was the so-called efficient public market really 'correct' to panic?

Insider Trading Rules, O.K.

You would be forgiven for thinking that public markets are transparent and private markets are secretive. But from an investor's perspective, the opposite is the case.

Because public companies can't reveal anything to anyone unless they reveal it to everyone (because otherwise it would be insider trading), the information they do release tends to be minimalist in content (though sadly, rarely in form).

By contrast, insider trading in private companies is perfectly legal. There is no requirement to be public with disclosures, and so, to private equity owners, portfolio companies are a completely open book.

Now, what do you think happens to an investor's perception of value during an exogenous shock when they have lots of information about a company compared to when they have very little? Would they be more or less likely to panic if they have very little insight into a company and its vulnerabilities?

The reason 'markets' get 'spooked' so easily isn't because they are so transparent. It's not because they know *so much*. It's because they know so little. And because they can do so little with what information they have. All they can really do is stick, twist or fold. Compare that to all the levers in the private equity arsenal. No wonder private equity is less volatile. It's not an accounting sleight of hand.

Incidentally, public markets haven't always been quite so strict. In London in the swinging 1960s, more than half the stock market was owned by individuals. They would buy their shares from a stockbroker in a pin-stripe suit and bowler hat, for high fees. The stockbrokers would normally be very familiar with the companies they were recommending, and much activity had 'a character that would today be regarded as insider trading'.[1] As the stock markets have become ever more focused on equal access and liquidity, rules intended to keep things fair have had the unintended consequence of making listed company reporting bland and intractable.

Do Illiquid Assets Outperform for Investors?

The question of whether this outperformance from illiquid assets translates into higher returns to the end-investor is more nuanced – because to a large degree, much of the outperformance is soaked up in fees – and this can be surprisingly complex to untangle in the numbers.

It does seem to be the case that private markets consistently outperform public markets – but speaking in such generalities, and about 'averages' and relative performance, is not, in my view, very helpful to the individual investor. Intermediaries obsess over relative performance because they are often judged against a benchmark. But ordinary people investing their only money care about *absolute* returns. In that regard, private markets funds have a good case to make...

Rather than listening to bold marketing claims or even hanging your hopes on historical data, it can be more revealing to look at some structural facts.

The main personal financial upside for private equity managers – the frontline barbarian – is carried interest (i.e. the 20% profit share in equity or 10% in credit). This typically also involves an 8% return hurdle for equity and 5% for credit – which means they do not receive a major proportion of their potential reward unless the fund as a whole (during its period of 'live' investment) provides a 5% or 8% per annum return, after all fees, to its investors.

Focusing on private equity for now: in any vintage (which just means the crop of funds that are raised in any given year), significantly more than half of private markets funds surpass this hurdle and 'achieve carry'. Even in the troubled vintage years of 2005–2008, when those funds were buying companies on the eve of the global financial crisis, Bain & Co. estimates that 60% of buyout funds achieved carry.

Even those funds that don't achieve carry rarely make an actual loss. They are just not surpassing 8% a year.

Serious investors don't commit to just a single fund, in one vintage, run by one manager. They will have a diversified private markets investment programme that will span many funds, across many vintages, many managers and many strategies and sub-asset classes. A diversified portfolio of private markets funds will include hundreds (or many thousands) of underlying companies or credits, and they are all actively managed and subject to this strong alignment of long-term interests between you and the manager, and on to the company executives and even employees. To achieve actual financial loss from such a portfolio held to maturity would require genius.

If I was invested in a diversified pool of private markets assets, across private equity, venture capital, private credit, some infrastructure and more, I might expect a decent double-digit percentage return, over time. Some years will be better than others, obviously. For instance, at the time of writing, the entire global private capital markets have been suffering with acute indigestion, unable (or more accurately, unwilling) to sell their rash of investments made at the turn of the decade because of persistently unfavourable macro-economic conditions. Eventually they will sell, and when they do, their investments will be old and they will probably have to accept valuations that were lower than they had anticipated. It won't show in the performance data for several years, but eventually these vintages will drag down the average – for a while at least.

At the same time, investment is not always a beauty contest – sometimes it's an ugly parade, a game of relative attractiveness. If private markets are not doing well, it is likely that everywhere is suffering at least as much.

One thing I would not hope or expect is to outperform the average private markets investors. On the contrary, I would expect my return to broadly reflect that average over time. This is not a book about how to be great at private markets investing. I'm not sure anybody is great at it. But everyone who approaches it sensibly and steadily will be where the real value is being created in the economy.

The promise of doing well by outperforming any market is a promise that will always be broken eventually. You want to be in a market where you can do well by *not* outperforming.

There Are No 'Star' Fund Managers

Hang on, what about *alpha*? Surely the top fund selectors will outperform the market – so why not 'select' them?

The idea of performance persistence – that a top performer is more likely to remain a top performer next time – is an enticing one.

For what it's worth, there is no correlation between past and future relative performance among *listed* equity funds. That is a case of monkey, meet dartboard. (Strange, then that public markets obsess over the cult of the 'star' fund manager.)

Private markets don't use such language. They prefer the less hyperbolic accolade of being 'top quartile.' The running joke is that every private markets manager professes to be top quartile. And the odd thing is, there might even be truth in it. If you survive long enough to have three funds, the chances are that one of them was top quartile. There is slightly more performance persistence in private equity than in public. This is probably to do with the long tail of poor performers, as well as a persistent advantage of scale for those at the very top of a growing industry. But as a fund selector, this does not really translate to meaningful performance persistence. The environment of private markets is too uncertain, and the timeframes between funds are too long. And then there is the problem of access. Unlike public markets, you can't just invest in whatever you like, whenever you like – they are privately negotiated agreements.

As a result, and in practice, no investor outperforms the private markets consistently. Not even the biggest and most experienced institutions. Beyond a certain level of diligence in order to weed out the obviously inferior fund managers, there are no 'winning strategies' in terms of fund selection.

This lack of performance persistence is also true at the level of so-called 'sub-asset-classes.' For a few years, big American buyouts can be the top performer. Then Asian venture capital. Then European mid-market private equity. Among big institutions investing in private markets, there is a maxim: don't time the market. (Just be in it.)

Instead, one should focus primarily on ensuring that the structure and approach to the market are sound: in terms of liquidity-matching, governance, alignment of incentives and diversification. Anything much beyond that is bravado.

This might sound like fatalism, but there is nothing fatalistic about putting in place sound governance that allows for the accountable and aligned delegation of duties right down the chain.

It's interesting to note that passive index investing in the stock market arises from a similar rationale – that you can't consistently outperform the market. But in that context, it has dire long-term consequences, because it breaks the chain of accountability, damaging governance and oversight on a systemic basis across the whole listed market.

Passive stock market investing was a reaction to the stock market fixation on alpha (the cult of the 'star' fund manager). It is a mindset of relative performance, a race to beat an ever-falling benchmark, since that is what public market intermediaries are judged upon – it is a classic race to the bottom.

By contrast, the barbarian fund manager is concerned only about absolute performance. Even if passive investing were to take off in private markets (and there are signs that it may) passive in this sense really means rules-based portfolios – the underlying funds and assets would still be actively managed.

Even engaged stock market players only really have one lever: to buy or sell. In private markets, the decision to commit is just the start of a very hands-on value creation process, and this is where fund investors add value. (There *is* considerable skill involved in *strategically managing* a portfolio of fund commitments – see Chapter 7 – and that is why investing in an independently managed fund-of-funds can be an attractive way into the market.)

Asness's Law

You may have spotted a disconnect between my characterisation of illiquidity as a driver of returns, and the fact that private markets' outperformance against their listed markets is not huge.

The simple explanation for this is best summed up by Cliff Asness, co-founder of AQR Capital Management. He quipped that, were an economic law to be named after him, it would be: 'there is no investment product so good *gross* that there isn't a fee that could make it bad *net*' [emphasis added]. 'Bad' is far too strong in this context (and the whole concept is obviously meant ironically). Even so, I would say there is a tendency for the huge gross outperformance of private markets to become something like 'almost equalised' with public markets once fees are accounted for. This means a huge amount of the product of the socio-economic value created by private markets is being eaten by the fund managers themselves. In buyouts, the spread between gross return and the net amount received by investors after fees is as high as 700 basis points.[2]

There is *some* justification for this – investing in private markets is an extremely resource-intensive activity. That's why the classic apples to oranges comparison of private markets managers to public markets managers makes the former look expensive. Anyone with an internet connection can invest in public equities. You can replicate the portfolio of some big fund manager in about half an hour. To replicate a private equity portfolio is impossible. The difference between transacting in private and public markets is the difference between fighting a hot war and playing *Fortnite*. Also, these fund managers take on very little of the role of the private markets general partner. They are little more than capital providers, so they are more like LPs, and they have just one lever: to transact. In a listed company, many GP functions are rolled up in the executive team and the board. To the largest degree, listed companies manage their own governance. But the salaries and costs would never be treated as fees.

The true cost of investment is not how much various labour providers might be getting. It is opportunity cost. What return do you actually get, and how does it compare with whatever else you can have invested in?

A focus on fees as a selection mechanism is an analysis that reminds me of the debunked Labour Theory of Value. The value of something is not the cost of producing it. Its value is determined by what it is worth to someone at the other end. And since private equity returns are in the form of real cash flow, that value is unequivocal.

But there is also a reason that this corner of the fund management industry has created more billionaires than perestroika. It's not just the carried interest/profit-share arrangement. The fees they charge can be absolutely enormous.

Not Just Hunters, but Gatherers

The headline terms of traditional private markets funds are remarkably sticky – i.e. they don't change much over time or between strategies or fund sizes. This makes a huge difference to a manager's income. The rule of thumb is that almost all private *equity* and venture capital managers get to charge roughly '2 and 20': a 2% per year management charge and

20% carried interest (the terms are different for other strategies, but they are similarly 'sticky').

There has been some finessing over the years, with some larger funds charging closer to 1.5% but 2–20 remains ballpark the case.

This stickiness has implications for alignment of incentives: it motivates fund managers to raise more capital, rather than simply make the best returns from whatever amount of capital is best suited to their strategy and skills. This is just because of the way the arithmetic works. A 1.5% management fee on a $150m fund is $2.25m a year – this is just to pay the staff and keep the lights on. The same fee on a $15bn fund is $225m – but they are still usually investing in about the same number of companies. The companies will be a lot bigger, so the task is a bit more complex and therefore costly but not a hundred times more costly. As a result, the absolute sum of the fee becomes incongruous with its original justification. On the other hand, as per Asness's Law, you would expect the most successful managers to be the ones able to attract the most capital and to charge the highest fees. In fact, the trend has been in the opposite direction to that which supply and demand would predict. The biggest managers, the ones who have been most successful and have gone on to raise ever larger funds, have gradually reduced their management fee from 2% to around 1.5%, and they've done so through something like etiquette or an acknowledgement of the principles of alignment and incentive underlying the terms of the traditional fund structure. But the fee reduction has not kept pace with the asset accumulation – not even close. There has also been movement in the other direction on other parts of compensation. For instance, some managers have increased their carried interest terms from the standard 20% to an antique 25% or even as high as 30%. Mr Asness, at least, might approve.

How Risky are Private Markets?

Oddly enough, while private markets managers will often play up the return potential, they also tend to overstate the risk.

In fact, anyone selling private markets tends to start by saying that obviously it's *high risk*... Think of the leverage! The illiquidity! But the returns are GREAT.

Venture capital? Super-risky, obviously. (But the outperformance 🏆!)

But it's all a big lie. And it's a very safe type of lie because it will never get anyone in trouble with the regulator. A lie that ensures that nobody will ever cherry-pick a failure and quote you out of context. A lie that ensures your compliance team will leave you alone, and you'll be known as a 'safe pair of hands', and they'll roll you out to do press interviews, and you'll get promoted.

But the truth that nobody will ever dare tell you is this: private market fund investing, in itself, is not especially risky.

Most people think of risk as the risk of losing their money from bad investments. From an appropriately diversified private markets portfolio, this is not a meaningful risk. Take buyouts: about 22% of buyouts lose some money. But only about 9% of buyout funds lose money. (In other strategies, fund loss ratios are 7% for private credit funds, 20% for venture funds and 25% for real estate.[3]) So if you go one more layer and have exposure to a diversified pool of such funds (and this can be achieved, for instance, with a single investment in a well-diversified 'fund of funds'), the risk is lower still – to below a 5% risk of loss for a well-structured portfolio.[4]

But there is another way of looking at risk – as missed opportunities. This can happen if you pay someone to put your capital at risk, but they don't.

They might over-diversify or buy expensive insurance, or simply avoid investment uncertainty wherever they can, which is the very domain of investment.

Why might this happen?

The 1967 Gene Wilder musical comedy, *The Producers*, told the story of two theatrical producers who hatch a scheme to defraud their investors by creating a musical that is designed to fail, because they notice you can guarantee a return from a flop by initially raising more than you need, whereas hits are much more. . . hit and miss. Of course, their production is so bad (camp-Nazis-and-Hitler-for-laughs) that it's good, and everything unravels. (It's literally an 'out' performance.)

Investors in theatrical productions were called 'angels'. They had to be – the risk of failure was so high. They were mainly wealthy patrons and they weren't paying producers to manage their risks, but to take them. Professional conduct on the part of the theatrical producers would necessarily include the assumption that the investor is *in it to win it* (the reverse of the Oedipal pact that is modern financial regulation).

Regulators are very attentive to 'risk-taking' – who is taking it, why, and what they are saying about it. But the endemic 'risk' for most investors in most regulated markets is the failure of those entrusted with their capital to take *sufficient* risk. It's what those CEOs of mid-20th century conglomerates were doing (or weren't doing) with investor's capital – diversifying their business in unproductive acquisitions in order to protect their own risk as individuals and agents. It's a tendency among stock-picking fund managers. They over-diversify or 'hug the benchmark', so that they don't deviate too far from it. They pretend to be taking risks and creating value on behalf of their investors while hugging their blue blanket like Gene Wilder, so as not to risk their salary and bonuses. Sober conservatism might be admirable in a solicitor, but if every agent that is paid to take measured risks chooses to diversify their personal risk, and that happens all the way down the chain, you end up depressing returns, blurring boundaries and incentives and ultimately, magnifying risk.

A private equity situation is not like this at all. The company executives are in a situation of significant risk and potential reward. For them, there is no escaping the full heat of that reality. They are a slave with one master and their fortunes are dependent on the outcome of that one company.

The private equity managers themselves are exposed to, perhaps, a dozen such deals in a fund and might have 'carry' in several funds at once, so they are exposed to less risk, since the underperformance of one poor deal will be diluted, so long as it doesn't dip them below the 8% hurdle.

By the next step down the line, things are much more diversified. LPs operating a consistent investment programme will have exposure to dozens of funds across many vintages. For individuals, such programmes can be replicated through feeder funds offered by private banks and investment platforms.

When pitching to big institutional investors, private equity managers rarely talk about risk. Not because the risk is so big or difficult to quantify or manage, but because most investors don't want or need it 'managed'. In this context, it's just not worth it, because the very structure of private markets investment partnerships takes care of operational risk.

In the context of a highly diversified portfolio of private markets funds, the risk-of-loss concept starts to lose its potency. We are no longer in the realm of extreme unquantifiable uncertainty, clinging for dear life above dire straits. We are in the sedate world of portfolio management and quantifiable risk. If you ask a pension fund manager to describe risk in private markets, they will often say something like, *a failure to reach our return targets*. And in this context, this is a reasonable response.

The Real Risk in Private Markets

So far, we've talked about the market risk of private investments. But there is another risk, and this one is far from trivial. On the rare occasion there is a blow-up of some retail fund, it is usually not because of bad performance – gradual losses are far less spectacular – but because of a liquidity mismatch in the fund's structure.

For investors to come properly unstuck, even though they may be in a diversified fund with minimal market risk, a manager needs to make a series of bad investments *without a fully committed source of funds*. If the underlying investments are less liquid than his capital base, there could be a rush to exit all at once, like panicking passengers on a sinking liner. This cascades through the fund structure, as the pressure on the narrow exit tips the liner on its side, and the captain tries to rapidly sell illiquid assets at discounts, further eroding values and confidence, until the whole thing capsizes.

There are certainly ways to invest in illiquid assets while retaining full investor liquidity – and we have looked at the most reputable in the previous chapters.

The irony of the liquidity mismatch risk is this: regulators and do-gooders insist that small investors need liquidity. But the more liquidity you attempt to build into an illiquid market, the more hidden risk you create. The fundamental return engine of private markets is illiquid. The true barbarian embraces this. The true barbarian actively limits their exposure to liquidity, sugar and tobacco. That is the best way to harvest the full 'illiquidity premium', live a long life, and do the right thing by your money. The listed private capital equivalent of this is to fully embrace the discount. What, you don't like buying things cheaply?

Generally speaking, the controls and safeguards that are built into private markets funds mean they can manage market risk head-on. Regulators and fund managers do nobody any favours by exaggerating investment risk, any more than you would be by exaggerating investment returns.

To the prospective investor, I would say this: of course, you can lose all your money in private markets, just like anywhere else. But it won't be a result of underlying investment performance, but because you have somehow departed from the system of aligned governance and committed capital provision thus outlined, without real diversification.

The main task with private markets investment isn't about managing market risk, it's about avoiding catastrophe by getting involved in bad governance and fund structures. For that, you have to pay attention to how you invest and who you invest with. *What* you invest in is a secondary matter and I would argue that has as much to do with taste as with risk or return.

12

Future Master of the Universe

> *. . . even in his lowest swoop the mountain eagle is still higher than other birds upon the plain, even though they soar.*
>
> – *Moby Dick*, **Herman Melville**

But maybe, you want *more*. You don't just want to invest *like* a barbarian – you want to *be* one. To actually venture out on the voyage of discovery and reap the fullest rewards.

If you have made it this far, you probably accept the power of private markets investment to create great wealth (it's hard to deny). But you will also have noted that, while passive investors benefit from this wealth creation effect, their outperformance compared to other ways they can invest is likely to be marginal-to-modest rather than perpetually *ripping* (but hey, marginal gains make a big difference over time).

The difference between this huge wealth creation and the modest net-returns for end-investors is the value soaked up by the barbarian class themselves. Wealth doesn't trickle down – it gushes, and then it trickles – so why not be at the very mouth of the cascade?

Broadly speaking, the wealth is soaked up in the following order:

- Private markets fund managers (primary funds)
- CEOs of portfolio companies
- Other senior managers and talent at portfolio companies
- Asset managers (providing feeder funds)
- Professional advisers around deals and value creation
- The end-investor

(On individual deals, the CEOs may be the biggest winners, but they are also often replaced, and not every deal will be a success. Successful barbarians, on the other hand, are repeat players across multiple bets. In addition, as a fund manager, the more capital you manage, the deeper the pool that sits at the top of the investment waterfall – fees that are paid out before investors, before preferred return and before carried interest.)

Let's look at how <u>you</u> can become a Future Master of the Universe.

'I have the Power'

If you are fairly early in your career, you can start at the bottom (which, like the Catskill eagle of this chapter's epigraph, would still put you higher than most).

The most common entry route is to get some experience of M&A or leveraged finance as an investment banking analyst and then positioning yourself to be poached by a private capital client, typically as an associate. This is the classic way into the larger managers (although bank bosses are getting ticked off with barbarians taking all their best young people, so they are tightening up their employment terms).

Some of the bigger managers are also setting up direct undergraduate analyst programmes, but the annual intake remains small. For instance, in the UK, industry stalwart 3i has historically run a very well-regarded grad programme.

Another classic stepping-stone is through the big management consultancies – this is particularly popular for private equity firms that focus on operational value creation and is therefore more common in the mid-market and growth capital. Given the importance of driving fundamental business value and the building out of internal value creation teams, this looks set to continue to be a growth area.

If you are already in finance, you might also consider a shiny MBA logo to increase your attractiveness. But beware: the top firms usually only take from a tiny number (often just one or two) Ivy League schools or equivalent. Also, it's becoming more common for private markets firms to hire first and then sponsor MBAs.

Aside from these standard avenues, there are some less conventional 'ways in' that could allow you to jump the hierarchy.

If you can demonstrate real domain expertise, this will make you stand out. I know successful barbarians that made it right to the top by starting out as physicians, software engineers, entrepreneurs and journalists. The tactical candidate might consider the different strategies taken by funds in the market and identify where their skills would be most prized, i.e. doctors would clearly be more appreciated in healthcare-focused funds, and so on. More than other managers, venture capital firms often prize experience over formal education – those who can demonstrate achievements and success, particularly as an entrepreneur.

Personality Spectrum – Unofficial Guide

Now this is about to get a little awkward – we need to talk about culture.

As a rule of thumb, the smaller the transaction, the greater the importance of specific individuals to the success of the deal. Conversely, the bigger the deal, the more impersonal the value drivers and the more replaceable are the specific individuals involved.

As a result, those professionals who tend to thrive in smaller deals, the mid-market, growth capital and venture capital, tend to have very strong social skills (in addition to many other competencies). By contrast, those who thrive in the world of larger transactions tend to be strongly left-brained, lack a certain warmth and less attuned to unspoken social cues. I spend much of my life defending private equity, in one way or another, and the social awkwardness (let's call it) of large buyout professionals does not always make this easy, because it can come across as arrogance or even rudeness. A classic complaint is of the barbarian in their early 30s bossing around a very senior CEO or CFO in their late-50s, without even the pretence of deference to their experience. (It's a personality trait that is no doubt echoed across the world of finance, but in private markets, you hold so much more power. . . .) Personally, I have nothing but sympathy for people who struggle in social contexts (no matter how financially successful they may be). While this is obviously a stereotype and will not relate to anyone in particular, at the level of firm-wide cultures, in my experience, it does tend to hold true.

The good news is, this means there is something for every personality type. Ruthlessly logical and like to be in control? Big LBOs or maybe private credit could be for you. Prefer partnering with people and taking some things on trust? Go small (you can still earn big).

Bear in mind that nothing is static – least of all, culture. If you set up your own fund (see below) or join a newer group, it could go on to scale into the larger cap space – this is how all today's mega funds started. The original barbarian fund, KKR's 1978 vehicle was $35m.

Ancillary and Advisory Roles

Much of the above pertains primarily to the most lucrative roles – those within investment teams. As you would expect, those doing the deals take the lion's share of the carried interest and income from fund management. But as private markets have grown, so too has the diversity of roles available – and the types of talent required.

To take one example, in recent years, numerous managers have begun hiring 'talent operating partners' – professionals with an HR or recruitment background – to support hiring within portfolio companies, designing compensation packages to fine-tune incentives and to put in place strong talent, training and development playbooks. Other new roles include in-sourcing AI, cyber-security and data experts, customer experience leaders, supply chain and procurement professionals and sustainability executives. In addition, most managers will have their own internal support services functions, such as HR, communications, marketing, investor relations, finance, compliance and legal.

'It doesn't matter what you do', my father used to say. 'Just do it close to the money'. You get the idea.

If you really play your cards right, from such support roles, you can still end up at the very top partnership table – particularly true for general counsel and COOs, for instance. I always envied a journalist contemporary of mine (he was slightly older and a lot smarter) who moved into investor relations (a role well-suited to good communicators). He ended up as a partner in a global manager. He also grew a long grey beard – I only mention this because, strange but true, even at 'peak beard' around 2022, private capital partners were pretty much 100% clean shaven.

And with this perfect segue, let me now comment on the sexes.

Women in Private Markets

Finance has historically been a male-dominated affair, but even in that context, private markets fund management was slow to attract the other 50% of humanity's talent pool.

The advisory community cottoned on first, particularly law firms and consultancies, but also investment banks. Bigotry and prejudice are the lazy conclusions to draw from this – and it's not for me to rule them out. But in my long observation of the market, this tardiness on the part of barbarians was largely down to structural reasons – particularly lengthy fund structures plus the very slow churn of employees within private capital firms.

Other reasons that are often cited include the well-documented tendency for men to be more attracted to risk-taking, and, perhaps, some women were also put off by the prospect of very long, anti-social hours.

Ironically enough, I'm not sure any of this accurately describes life as a private markets executive.

For one thing – as we have seen – private markets investment is not the hyper-risky undertaking of popular perception (with the exception of doing individual venture capital deals). Second, while fund managers are no slouches, the cadence of work is actually somewhat accommodating to family life. When you are 'on a deal', then it's truly full-on. But when you aren't – and this can be for extended periods – investment professionals actually have a lot of freedom and flexibility. They are also compensated sufficiently well to cover frenzied deal periods with some high-quality domestic support.

For several years, I advised an organisation dedicated to attracting women to private markets, called Level20. They have worked hard to explain the realities of the various roles in private markets, to connect young female professionals with (male and female) mentors in the industry, and to encourage women to stay on for senior roles – with great success. Today, 15% of senior roles in private equity firms are held by women, and there is a much larger representation throughout the wider teams.

External Advisers

You don't have to be an employee of a fund manager to do well. On the wealth creation gravy train, external advisers might not be in first class, but they have plenty of extra legroom. First-year private equity lawyers at top firms can earn more than the salary of many heads of state. The big four accounting firms, which individually enjoy higher annual income than the GDP of many countries, count private markets fund managers as major sources of revenue, both from traditional tax, accounting and audit services, as well as transaction advisory and consulting. Private markets managers tend to be relatively thinly resourced and are used to bringing in outside expertise. Indeed, there are many more people making a fine living advising private capital firms than there are fund management professionals themselves.

And you don't have to be at some 'magic circle' firm to benefit – there's plenty of room at the bottom too (it's 'winner take most' type situation). Whatever area your business expertise is in, there is likely to be a fund somewhere that wants to know what you know. I once asked a sector-generalist buyout professional how they find niche, domain-specific advisers. He told me they go on to Amazon and literally 'hire the guy that wrote the book'. I'll let you know.

Emerging Barbarians

The bottom-up nature of private markets investment means there will always be room for small, agile managers who are able to claim a competitive advantage in a certain niche. A steady stream of fund management start-ups come online each year, and for the aspiring barbarian who walks to the beat of their own drum, this route could be attractive. It would certainly be bold.

The good news is that, to a degree, the investment establishment is on your side – or at least, it's not systemically against you. Various investment institutions, from large pension plans to funds-of-funds managers, have specific programmes or allocations for investing in new private markets firms. The industry term for such start-ups is 'emerging managers', which can mean anything from a true start-up to a manager on their third fund. In each case, they still have something to prove – they are not yet regarded as a 'brand-name manager'. Given that accessing the best funds is not always easy for investors, it's a wise strategy for large investment programmes to have their fingers in many smaller pies, in the hope that one will become a big manager of tomorrow.

Few start-ups can afford to be too choosy about who they take money from, but remember – the aim of the game is to build long-term commitments with partners who believe in you. Whether you are raising money deal-by-deal, for a mini-fund or a fully-fledged 10-year GP/LP structure, it's going to be a journey, with ups and downs, and hopefully 're-ups' (new commitments) or at least 're-downs' (a smaller commitment than the previous fund).

Joe Briggs of BCF is a reformed funds lawyer turned capital formation adviser to emerging managers. 'Look for investors that have a connection or affinity with your strategy or niche, and work out if what you're offering them will be additive to their portfolio', he says. 'Find ways to build long-term relationships with these investors – get to know them, encourage them to get to know you, and deliver on the things you say you will do,' he advises.

Family offices can make good seed investors for this reason (particularly if you happen to already manage one). Bottom line – you need capital, but ideally it will be from people who really 'get you' and believe in you early on in the process.

Essential Qualifications to Raise a Fund

There are none. Seriously. In most of the financial world, you can't sneeze without checking with the regulator or some self-appointed professional standards body. But anyone can raise a private capital fund and invest it – and I do mean anyone. You will usually need to register with the relevant authority, but it's not like you are asking to practice medicine or fly a passenger jet. Okay, if you have previous convictions for financial fraud, you won't get authorised. But non-financial criminal activity (vandalism, barbarity) – probably okay.

Of course, if you want to get a top private equity *job*, qualifications *are* necessary. But they are exactly that – qualifiers for employment. It is surely helpful to have an MBA or to have worked at JP Morgan, but these things are (somewhat) arbitrary filters that allow private equity employers to rapidly exclude their over-supply of applications. They aren't the keys to success in private markets. For that, there is really just one barrier: capital. And to attract it, you need *credibility*.

The easiest way to have credibility is to already be a successful private capital professional, who is scratching an entrepreneurial itch by setting up a new outfit. Or maybe you've just done a few of your own self-financed, entrepreneurial bootstrapped deals and are ready for external funding.

Even so, there should probably be more to it than that – after all, if investors are going to back something unproven, it must have an 'x' factor.

A credible proposition will usually be a team with some demonstrable deal-making skills (frustrated former investment bankers often give it a go). And increasingly, investors are looking for less obviously finance-related angles – perhaps business operators who understand a specific sector or secular opportunity, or maybe they are technicians or academics poised to exploit an exciting new theme, such as science PhDs in early-stage venture biotech, data scientists in AI growth equity, or ex-founders and CEOs in mid-market buyouts.

If you manage to raise the capital (it won't be easy) and you really do have a plan (you know where to source good businesses and how to improve – and scale them fast), then you might get very rich. At least, you are no more or less likely to fail than any other private markets manager. After all, investment success is not a formula. It's a rarefied air at the top of private capital, but in the end, everything comes down to investment returns. You may have a dozen plush offices in global capitals all staffed with top MBA graduates: a run of duff deals, and it all ends. Not spectacularly – failed managers don't blow-up, they just fade away, like old soldiers are said to do. Or as Joe Briggs puts it: 'Anyone who says "life is short" has clearly never been an LP investor at the tail end of an underperforming closed-ended private investment fund'.

That's why investors are always looking for the next big thing – because things change and nobody knows what the 'new guard' will look like. In fact, as they say in Hollywood, 'nobody knows anything'. But that also means anybody has a shot at making it big. So, my advice would be, if you have the urge and think you have the edge, why not give it a try?

It turns out, the price of entry into the world's most exclusive capitalist club is at once both extremely high, and basically a mirage.

For insight into becoming a barbarian, career progression and setting up your own fund, scan this QR code.

13

The Social Utility of Barbarians

Outside of the investment world, the reputation of private markets – and private equity, in particular – could be better, to say the least. It is an easy target for sensational journalism, and social media is awash with criticism. Go on to YouTube and search for 'private equity' – most videos are hostile. So, the question you might ask is why this is the case and whether your investment in private markets will actually be good for the world. . .

The psychologist Jordan B Peterson has asserted that, rather than defending your reputation, you should act in such a way that you merit a good one. It is surely wise advice – for individuals. Unfortunately, I'm just not sure it applies to the corporate sphere.

In my experience, there is no correlation between a company's or a sector's ethical conduct and its broader public reputation. There could even be a reverse correlation.

Medicines are widely trusted, and yet (or because) regulatory and institutional capture by multinational pharmaceutical companies is endemic. Chemical companies are all but invisible to the public, just like their toxins that saturate our environment. They have armies of lawyers and scientists dedicated to avoiding health and environmental concerns.

Big tech is generally seen as a force for good, while it employs the brightest minds to work out how to enslave the youngest minds through addictive, dopamine-saturating content. Advertising by sugar companies, aka big food, has successfully convinced the consumer that industrial by-products really have *mamma's home-cooked goodness*. Everyone from Donald Trump to Warren Buffett gives Coca-Cola endless endorsement, and yet sugar is almost certainly a bigger cause of disease and early death than tobacco.

Ethics are an inherently personal matter, so you may not agree with the examples I have chosen, but hopefully you can accept the broad principle at play.

Private markets – and private equity, in particular – don't play this game. Or at least, it plays it very badly. These firms don't generally advertise. They don't engage in regulatory capture (not, I suspect, out of ethical concerns, but because they just don't have the bureaucratic apparatus that makes this possible). Most of the people working in private markets are left-hemisphere-oriented thinkers. They tend to be hyper-rational and not usually the most empathic. They assume logical argument will prevail and that's why their political advocacy is less effective than their wallets would suggest.

Most of the criticism online is partial or ill-informed. At the same time, private equity isn't perfect, and some of the criticisms have more than a kernel of truth. The question is whether their criticism is damning of the model itself.

The Healthcare Problem

A surprisingly large proportion of criticism about private equity at the moment is about dentistry. Just look online at the comments sections, and you'll see what I mean.

The general complaint is that people's dentists, under private equity ownership, have begun to aggressively push products and even procedures that seem unnecessary. It is not difficult to see how the logic of private equity incentives could lead to this. My local dentistry is owned by a private equity firm (one that I happen to know personally), and I have experienced this phenomenon first hand.

But the first step to fixing a problem is proper diagnosis, and this is not a private equity-specific problem.

Healthcare is a sector where commercial and ethical motives most obviously diverge. In an advanced society, there will naturally be very few sick people. Profit-motivated actors are therefore incentivised to create illness and dependencies, to ignore simple solutions (such as improvement of diet), to advocate for complex procedures, for novel on-patent drugs over cheap off-patent drugs or natural remedies and to ignore side effects that may create proliferating demand for interventions. If anything, the situation is worse in state medicine, because the role of the private sector remains huge but behind-the-scenes. I am not aware of any easy solution to this except a greater focus on professional conduct and high ethical standards. I merely make the point that it is not a private equity-specific issue. It is endemic across healthcare – but it is normally much worse. If more people understood how the pharmaceutical sales machine worked, they would be shocked. Their funding of the medical conferences, events, panels, journals, travel and yes, even regulatory bodies and regulators themselves, utterly compromises the practice of medicine, but since the price of drugs rarely faces off directly to the consumer, while the average citizen's knowledge of drug trials is minimal, it all goes largely unnoticed. I am yet to come across a private equity firm that seeks to rig the entire system the way that many multinationals habitually do. Indeed, I suspect private equity is structurally incapable of doing so.

In the case of dentistry, it is the responsibility of private equity firms to make good returns. It is the responsibility of dentists to fix teeth and make a living. Each has its duties, its ethically binding obligations. In some cases, as in this case, there may be tension between the two, and that is a signal that there is an ethical dimension. The professional conduct of dentists appears to be failing. You might say, *ah that's because of the false incentives put in place by private equity*. But private equity is merely putting in place commercial incentives, which is a characteristic of the private sector and the free market in general, not private equity. For medical professionals, the professional code must come first.

On Asset Stripping

Another common criticism of private equity is that they are asset strippers. This is a weaker claim. Asset-stripping is a loaded term, but context is everything.

In an advanced economy, you would expect a high degree of asset specialisation. Airports don't own airlines. Airlines don't own their aeroplanes. Aeroplane owners don't usually own the engines in the aeroplanes. And the same is true for hospitals and medical equipment, factories and so on. Such asset leasing models lead to operationally agile, capital-light businesses, better capital allocation and greater efficiency.

At the other extreme, there are investors who buy companies only to sell off the parts. This was Richard Gere's job in the film *Pretty Woman*, and in an economy full of bloated companies, it serves a social function, just as the breaking up of the 1970s conglomerates drove US corporate efficiency and prosperity. But in a world where there is a management consultant on every street corner, most businesses are pretty well optimised – there is not much to strip.

But asset-stripping does still exist. I have come across some independently wealthy entrepreneurs who do this. They buy badly performing asset-heavy businesses, but rather than try to revive them, they close the business down, pay off the workers and sell off the assets. Perhaps this also serves a legitimate function, but it's not something institutional private equity players do. Their first motive is always to sell a going concern.

The only clearly egregious form of asset-stripping is that motivated by profit extraction at the expense of a business that would otherwise have survived. The difficulty is that to make the accusation stick, you usually have to prove a negative. In reality, situations that could be suspected of asset-stripping are extremely rare in private equity. Where they do occur, it is typically in 'turnaround' investments – a specialist activity of acquiring businesses that are already distressed, and where survival without the private equity investment would have been unlikely.

One tactic that deserves to be singled out is the practice of buying retailers for the value of their property portfolio, then selling it off and leasing it back – leaving the operating business vulnerable to the next consumer downturn. What can be a legitimate tool in some industries can just be foolish in more cyclical ones. The 2003 buyout of Debenhams in the UK is often cited as an example of this. The private equity firms made a strong return, sold the business back to the stock market, and later, the business collapsed. But it was much later. . . some 13 years, so the causality is rather murky. And who is to say that a tired old retailer really was the best owner of the valuable property portfolio, from an economic productivity point of view? Retailers are very publicly prominent, but why is it less legitimate to use the properties for offices, hotels or data centres?

It's also worth considering that such practices do not describe 'private equity' – anyone can do them, and indeed the most heinous examples of this practice are not usually found within organised private equity. For example, in the United Kingdom, British Home Stores was a high street staple until it was bought by Sir Philip Green, who paid his wife billions in dividends in the good years, and sold off the property portfolio without reinvesting in the company's pension scheme. He finally sold it to a former bankrupt for £1, with the loss of 11,000 jobs.

As much as I've played up the disruptive role of private equity so far, the truth is, they have always had one foot in the corporate establishment. Almost immediately, back in the early 1980s, private equity refrained from making hostile bids for companies to ensure they didn't upset their LPs, who were pension funds and insurance companies – fully embedded in the mainstream corporate system. A private equity firm that went around asset-stripping like the above example would never raise another dime from a pension fund. In truth, they are somewhat tame, these barbarians.

★

There are certainly instances when private equity managers will be faced with a failing business and an ethical dilemma between stripping out whatever they can from the remains of the business – and so fulfilling their fiduciary responsibility to investors – or using whatever assets are left to give more generous redundancy pay-outs (for instance). It is a somewhat hypothetical scenario, but it is not uncommon, and I suspect, in general, barbarians normally lean towards their fiduciary responsibilities.

Toys 'R' Us Goes Bust

Another enormous amount of online criticism of private equity centres on one deal: the collapse of Toys 'R' Us. The claim is that the company was over-leveraged, and so it failed, resulting in bankruptcy and the loss of 33,000 jobs. This is pretty much the case. The question is what lessons to draw from it. Is it representative of private equity per se?

Statistically speaking, no – such failures, particularly on this scale, are very rare.

Logically speaking, would the mismanagement of a single publicly listed company be an indictment of the stock markets in general? Obviously not.

But if I had lost my job, I would be angry, because the financial structure of this deal does look stupid, and I don't think that's just with the benefit of hindsight. Retail is highly cyclical, and the digital threat was apparent at the point of purchase.

But you can't legislate against stupidity, you can only ensure that there are no rewards for failure. The dealmakers behind Toys 'R' Us did not 'asset-strip'. They did not pay their wives super dividends. Rather, they invested in store refurbishments, improved supply chain tech and attempted to boost the Babies 'R' Us brand, which was profitable for a time. But ultimately, it didn't pay off. The world was moving away from physical retail outlets.

And then consider this: before the buyout, Toys 'R' Us had been listed on the stock exchange, and it had been struggling. Its sales had flatlined for years; it had expensive overheads and it had done an early deal with Amazon but then got caught up in a lawsuit after Amazon started working with competitors. It was a real mess. Even so, the buyout shops paid stock market investors a 60% premium to acquire the business. So now you know why the deal had so much leverage: because extractive public market shareholders and intermediaries made out like bandits, while the private equity investors took on a big challenge to revive the business against all odds – and it didn't work out.

I'm not proposing the above as a definitive judgement on the ethics of that particular deal, (I'm sure there is plenty of blame to share around), only that, even in such exceptional cases, which appear blatantly irresponsible at first glance, are rarely so simple.

Private Equity Is a Sin-eater

For the most part, private equity's reputation suffers the Batman/anti-hero phenomenon: the vigilante good guy tainted by the very corruption only he can address.

In boardrooms these days, there isn't much difference between 'optics' and ethics. If it looks good and sounds good, *it is* good. This makes it easier for companies to conflate reputation-management with ethical action. A whole PR industry has been created under the rubric of something called ESG to argue precisely that: that companies never need to sacrifice profits in order to act ethically, because over a long enough time horizon, the two will converge.

You don't have to be a moral philosopher to realise it is a logical fallacy.

Morality is not doing the right thing because it will benefit you (also known as 'enlightened self-interest'). Morality is doing the right thing, full stop. It is doing the right thing even when it has bad 'optics' – such as cutting jobs or relocating factories or disrupting entire industries. The reason private equity can often make so much money from de-listing public companies is that such hard decisions very often just can't be taken in the full glare of public disclosure. The optics of allowing a company to die slowly are so much better than taking hard ethical actions to salvage what is of value and enable regrowth.

Private equity lobby groups focus on how many jobs are created under private equity ownership. It's understandable. But it's an error because it is asking to be judged on results that you don't judge yourself against. A deal that creates a big return but no new jobs or even net-negative employment is better than a deal that creates jobs but a poor return – or a loss. Any implication otherwise is disingenuous. If Microsoft, Google or OpenAI were judged on their *quantifiable* net impact on jobs across the global economy, they would be outlawed immediately. We tolerate them because we accept that progress only happens through creative destruction.

You might say, what about the worker who isn't exceptional. Isn't private equity elitist? It reminds me of a restructuring at a company, where management told HR: 'headcount will halve, IQ will double'. It's an extreme example, but the hard truth is that there is no choice other than to pursue productivity and competence. If you do that, everyone has a chance of finding a place in a vibrant, diverse society. The alternative is to level everyone and everything down to the point where there is no division, no value-distinction, no judgement, no diversity. Down there, at zero degrees Kelvin, where things are much more certain, because atoms no longer vibrate, hearts no longer beat, roses no longer smell and everything is truly equal.

It's difficult to do good in the world without engaging with some dysfunction, and by trying to address it, one is associated with it. And it's very difficult to change the world for the better without taking on powerful incumbents and vested interests. That means, to do good, both the weak and the powerful will end up disliking you.

Even venture capital makes more enemies than friends – there are a hundred-odd entrepreneurs turned down by venture capital for every one that gets funded. And many of the CEOs who make it that far will still subsequently get fired or simply fail. Popularity is a numbers game, as is politics. Ethical action is qualitative.

Private Equity Is a People Business

The real leverage that private equity firms use is not debt but the ability to fire the CEOs and top leaders in the businesses they own. And they do it *a lot*. To the casual observer, this is perhaps evidence of a casual, dismissive treatment of individuals. But there is another way of looking at it. Only an investor who values individual contributions would put so much emphasis on getting the *right* people.

One of the big judgements a private equity firm makes about companies is around their culture. It doesn't feature much in the commentary or analysis on private equity because it's very difficult to quantify, but this people-factor is integral to the asset-class. And they often pay great attention to this during the life of an investment.

It is easy to look people-friendly, compassionate, progressive when all you do is manipulate people's lives from afar – with algorithms, taxes, mercantilism, insurance premiums, interest rates, advertising and lobbying. But structures like private equity must contend with actual individuals. They must value them as people, appreciate them, speak to them, judge them, incentivise them, look them in the eye and, if necessary, fire them. They are involved in people's lives, with all their messiness, oppression and advantage, hopes and fears, risks and rewards. In other words, it's the real world. And as with any other part of the economy, people can be treated both well and poorly by private equity. The morality of any given situation almost always sits well beneath whatever framework that's put in place, at the level of individual decisions. Private equity is a system that tends to reward ethical action financially over the long term. Mistakes will be made, and 'a few bad apples' is a fact of life – it is not a perfect system. Cherry-picking an isolated failure is therefore not particularly instructive as to the impact of private equity per se.

When Gross Returns Matter

Much academic criticism of private equity relates to fees, and in that context, gross numbers tend to be derided as purely marketing. But what matters to society is not net returns, but the value created out there in the real world, which is measured by gross returns. In this context, the question of how that payback is split between the people managing the investments and their passive investors is subordinate.

To measure the value that the private equity model contributes to society, the return is the last place most people look, when it should be the first. And not just the fund's gross returns. If there were no private equity bidders, asset prices for small and medium-sized companies would plummet, further shrinking the benefits of setting up and running enterprises and all the knock-on effects that would have on employment and productivity.

Bad Reputation, Good Sign

If anything, were the reputation of private equity to suddenly improve, I would take it as a warning sign. The faithful fulfilment of their duties will always create powerful enemies. The rise of engaged, patient corporate ownership will be a perennial threat to those who control the pillars of the corporate establishment: unions, regulators, the media, politicians, not to mention those within the corporate world with a vested interest in the status quo.

The controversy and resulting vigilance surrounding private equity are as much of a comfort to me as the complacency around other sectors is concerning: the labour conditions maintained by the fashion industry; the slave labour tolerated by the fishing and restaurant industry and the child slave labour wilfully ignored by the renewable energy industry.

Perhaps, to be loathed is merely the fate of anything that saves a corrupt system from itself. The agents of progress often have a sacrificial aspect; maybe that's why doing the right thing takes a certain level of integrity, detachment – perhaps even insensitivity.

But unlike sacrificial heroes, private equity managers are co-beneficiaries of their successes. They are not masters of the universe or barbarians at the gates. They are just plain old economic agents.

I am not defending any party. I am defending a model of value creation that has much to offer the world. It can be watered down from within, regulated from without and misjudged and misunderstood by all. Or it can be put to work for the commonwealth.

Conclusion

What might be the longer term consequences of increasing the participation of individual investors in private markets?

Individuals will have exposure to returns that are better correlated with the productive economy. Meanwhile, their absolute returns are likely to be better than otherwise; and even this effect is only somewhat marginal, marginal gains compound over time.

Individual investors may even make private markets more efficient, more liquid and (even) less volatile than they are now. That's because most institutional investors share similar pressures in times of stress – they will often have targets about the proportion of private markets assets they can hold relative to public assets, so if the value of public market assets collapse, this can create a rebalancing problem (known as the denominator effect). Funds powered by individual investors can benefit from such structural dislocations by buying assets on the secondary market, which will, in turn, drive up prices of secondaries (which will be good for institutions too). In this sense, individual investors may further remove systemic pressures and risks from the system.

On the flip side, a theoretician might point out that the more capital that flows into private markets, the lower the returns must go. This assumes that investment returns are static, like a pie to be divided up. It's similar to the *lump of labour* fallacy: the belief that there's a fixed number of jobs in the economy, so one worker's gain must be another's loss. But economies are dynamic systems and new capital can transform the potential of a sector, funding better infrastructure, unlocking efficiencies, building out complementary ecosystems and enabling entirely new business models. This is especially true in private markets, where the boundaries of the opportunity-set are undefined. I would therefore be less concerned that this revolution will depress returns – particularly for the foreseeable future, given that individuals continue to constitute a small proportion of the overall funding base.

Other consequences could be that, over time, the power of a few very large LPs – often, in practice, bureaucrats or state-appointed intermediaries – will diminish, as private markets managers diversify their funding base. This will be replaced by a more fragmented investor base, akin to those on the stock market – or literally as such. Ironically, this could prompt the rise of a new privileged, insufficiently accountable investment elite but this time emanating from private markets itself.

There is a view of investment that says, eventually, everything bends back to the public markets. If that is true, it is in everyone's interests to ensure that stock markets work as effectively as possible, with the highest standards of governance, meaningful disclosure and the responsible exercise of investors' rights and duties. We are a very long way from this. I choose to believe there will be a tipping point in the growth of private markets that will force public market intermediaries and regulators to act to improve stock markets as a better home for companies. In the meantime, having balanced exposure between the two markets seems a sensible plan.

★

Private markets are controversial, not because they use new, complex, systemically risky, esoteric instruments. They are controversial because they are a return to real investment, that is slow, somewhat cumbersome, diligent, personal, bespoke, un-optimised, decentralised and lightly regulated. They are vehicles of upward social mobility, wealth creation and ultimately, wealth spreading. Private markets partnerships are inclusive institutions, and their effect should be similar to that of the ancient commenda.

There is always a wariness towards such socially progressive institutions, because they threaten the status quo and those who already have power. But when enough people take a stake in the productive potential of their economies, everyone wins. Sometimes it takes a barbarian to prevent the decline and fall.

If this makes private markets investment sound overly altruistic, I make no apology. There is nothing in it for you *immediately*. It takes patience. You are not doing it for you, you are doing it for future-you, and there is not much difference between that person and other people, in your family, your community and your society.

Becoming a barbarian is a mindset. With at least a portion of your wealth, you must choose to step outside of the regulated casino, the always-on, no-commitment, dopamine-fuelled digital trading floor, the race-to-the-bottom passivity, the race-to-mediocrity search for cheapness or 'value', the padded guard rails of monopolistic income and instead, choose real *investment*.

The Implications of Democracy

The opening up of private markets is often called a 'democratisation'. Democracy requires oversight and participation, or it descends into quiet tyrannies – obeying the form of democracy and good governance, but through lack of attention, not the fact of it. It is a truism that the greater your blind trust in a system, the less worthy of your trust it will become.

Bureaucrats, intermediaries and fiduciaries dominate the investment landscape. Their interests are not yours, and unless held accountable, they will diverge ever more over time. Some will say that investment markets are just too large, complex and specialised for such individual oversight. I disagree. The task of governance and oversight is, by definition, the task of every citizen. I would say governance of their own capital investments is the least expectation of citizens in a modern society.

Admittedly, with investment markets so abstracted and indexed, and portfolios diversified and fractionalised to the point that the very concept of ownership becomes effaced, this duty certainly does seem unfeasible.

The democratisation of private markets is an opportunity to bring investment back down to earth. The variety of funds, the grassroots nature of many strategies, the thematic and regional diversity of options – all this is an opportunity for investors to choose (at least for part of their portfolio) investments that are not remote or abstracted, but grounded in real business activity.

There is a utopian fantasy where everyone would just invest directly in their local communities and businesses. But there is a dystopian equivalent – where it is the sovereign wealth funds of foreign, sometimes totalitarian states that extract the economic benefit from your economy, while you and your fellow citizens invest your savings for no real return, in sovereign bonds, to fund their centralised expenditures – on everything from roads to 'defence' arsenals. The latter is closer to the current state of affairs than many realise.

If you would prefer to have a stake in the economic success, productivity and prosperity of your own communities, in accordance with values you can connect with, I would say private markets – however you choose to access them – will be worth your time and consideration.

Investments can be complicated but good governance and oversight needn't be. It is about identifying principles that you stand by and ensuring they are met. Principles like alignment of interests, a belief that investment itself is not zero-sum and that your capital can actually do some good and that commitment *itself* is a source of value.

You can have the best ideas, the greatest potential and the longest lever in the universe, but without a strong and stable fulcrum, they will be worthless.

You are the fulcrum.

Welcome to the world of private markets.

THE END

About the Author

Ross Butler has spent 25 years involved with the private capital industry, as a journalist, policy adviser and consultant. Today he is host of the Fund Shack private capital channel and podcast, and advises leading investment firms on governance, policy, ethics and communication. He has held industry-level roles, including Secretary of the Professional Standards Committee of the EVCA (now Invest Europe); Directorship at LPEC, the Listed Private Capital Association; and Editor of Real Deals, when he was awarded Private Equity Journalist of the Year (2005, 2006, and 2008).

You can connect with Ross here: http://q-r.to/Ross-Butler

Glossary of Terms

A

Absolute return: A return measure that is not relative to a benchmark or comparator – it's just what you got back relative to what you put in.

Accredited investor: A bureaucratic definition of an individual investor that differs by jurisdiction, typically indicating higher-end 'mass affluent' individuals and upwards, and often requires demonstration of some investment knowledge

Acquisition: Buying control or ownership of a company.

Agency, problem: The misalignment of interest that can occur when a company is run by agents who don't have a meaningful ownership stake.

Alternative investments: Term sometimes used to refer to private markets (to distinguish them from public markets). Often slightly more expansive – can include things like hedge funds and forestry.

Asset based lending: A corporate loan secured against physical assets

Asset backed finance: Loans issued against a pool of assets, often securitised. Can be consumer loans, mortgages, etc.

Asset stripping: Selling off a company's assets, potentially harming its long-term viability.

B

Barbarian: A term used in this book, and occasionally in pop culture, for a private markets fund manager.

Barbarians at the Gate: Term popularised by the eponymous 1989 bestseller describing the leveraged buyout of RJR Nabisco by KKR; now associated with private equity firms.

Basel III: International regulatory accord introduced post-GFC, imposing stricter capital requirements on banks, thereby significantly increasing the opportunity for private credit funds.

Business Development Company (BDC): US investment structure created in the mid-20th century to allow public investors to access private, middle-market corporate debt and equity.

Buy-and-build: A private equity strategy involving the acquisition of one company (a "platform") followed by further acquisitions ("add-ons") to create operational synergies, geographic expansion and multiple arbitrage opportunities.

C

Cashflow: Earnings, less expenses, interest payments, tax.

Carried interest: The fund manager's share of profits, typically 20%, paid only if certain performance thresholds (hurdle rate) are met. Also called 'carry'.

Closed-end fund: Funds with a fixed number of shares. After an initial fundraising or subscription period, does not continually raise new capital or redeem capital.

Co-investment: Investment alongside a private equity fund manager typically without additional management fees or carried interest, but with passive investor status.

Commenda: A medieval partnership agreement, involving a stay-at-home capital provider ('commendator') and a travelling merchant ('tractator'), profit-sharing, limited liability, and a finite lifespan, structurally resembling modern private equity limited partnerships.

Commitment: An investor's obligation to provide a certain amount of capital to a fund manager, on-demand.

Continuation fund: A specialised single-asset fund allowing a fund manager to extend ownership of a valuable asset beyond the original fund's life, offering investors an opportunity to maintain exposure.

Creative destruction: Joseph Schumpeter's theory describing capitalism's dynamic, relentless renewal through innovation and disruption, underpinning private markets' social utility.

D

Deal flow: The number of investments a manager completes, or the number of serious opportunities that flows through its selection funnel.

De-list: Acquiring the shares in a public company and remove it from the stock market, into private ownership. Also called 'take-private' or 'public-to-private'.

Democratisation (of private markets): A trend whereby regulatory changes and structural innovations allow individual investors – not just large institutions – to participate in private market investments.

Discount to NAV (Net Asset Value): The phenomenon of closed-end investment companies trading below the published value of their underlying assets, common in listed private capital vehicles. The corollary – 'premium to NAV' – is a rarity.

Distribution: Capital returned to investors in a closed-end fund.

Dividend recapitalisation (dividend recap): A private equity practice involving taking on new debt to pay dividends to investors during ownership.

DPI (distributed-to-paid-in): A measure of the total distribution to date as a proportion of the total capital actually paid in. It is net of fees and carried interest and is sometimes called the 'cash-on-cash' return.

Drawdown: The capital that is committed but not yet called by a fund manager. Or the process of calling it.

Due diligence: Legalistic term for assessing the quality of an investment opportunity or assessing the veracity of available information.

E

Evergreen funds: Evergreens are generally open-ended funds without a fixed termination date. Instead of liquidating and distributing all capital at the end of a fund life, they recycle proceeds and continue investing.

Equity: Ownership interest in a company.

F

Financial engineering: The application of financial techniques (such as debt leverage or structuring) to enhance investment returns; frequently associated with leveraged buyouts.

Fund-of-funds: Closed-end fund that invests in other closed-end LP funds. Often take advantage of primary, secondary, or co-investment opportunities, thereby offering rapid diversification and simplifying allocation complexity.

G

Gated evergreen: Term used in this book to refer to listed or unlisted open-ended perpetual investment vehicles with shares that are contingently redeemable.

General Partner (GP): The fund manager or entity responsible for raising capital and actively managing a private markets fund, bearing responsibility for identifying and managing investments.

Growth capital: Private equity investment into profitable, high-growth businesses, often for a minority stake.

Guerrilla: A term used in this book for an investor or fund manager who opportunistically invests in private markets secondary transactions, co-investments, continuation funds, GP stakes and other non-primary opportunities to capture tactical advantages.

H

High-yield bonds: Debt finance used for LBOs, in the form of 'senior subordinated notes', not secured against company assets and therefore attract higher interest rates.

Hurdle rate: The minimum return (often 8% for equity funds, 5% for credit) required before a GP receives any carried interest.

I

Illiquidity premium: The return investors earn as supposed 'compensation' for locking capital into illiquid investments. A fallacy.

IPO: Initial public offering – the sale of a company's share on the stock market for the first time.

IRR: Internal rate of return. The annual percentage return a closed-end fund has delivered, taking into account not just how much money is made, but also when it is paid back to investors. Easy for fund managers to fiddle.

Interval funds: Open-ended, evergreen vehicles allowing investors limited periodic liquidity, commonly quarterly, and designed to offer direct private markets exposure without the complexities of closed-end fund structures.

J

J-curve: In a closed-end fund, what the value of your capital and commitment looks like when plotted on a graph – early losses before any returns are made but fees are charged, and later gains.

Junk bonds: Derogatory (and somewhat archaic) name for high-yield bonds.

L

Leveraged buyout: An acquisition technique where a company is bought primarily using debt (and some equity) secured against the cashflows, and sometimes assets, of the target company.

Limited Partner (LP): Passive investors providing capital to a private market fund, traditionally large institutions or high-net-worth individuals.

Limited partnership: Legal form (in the Anglosphere) of the classic closed-end 10-year private markets fund.

Liquidity mismatch: A structural risk arising when a fund offers investors short-term redemption rights despite holding long-term illiquid assets, potentially leading to redemption pressures and forced asset sales.

M

Management buyout: Structurally very similar to an LBO, but with a greater emphasis on the existing management team becoming co-owners of the business alongside a private equity acquirer. Usually refers to buyouts of small and middle market companies.

Merchant banking: Historical practice involving private partnerships lending their own capital directly to merchants and enterprises.

Multiple arbitrage (Valuation leverage): A strategy exploiting the tendency of larger companies to attract higher valuation multiples than smaller companies, enabling private equity investors to profit by increasing the scale of portfolio companies.

N

NAV (Net Asset Value): The total market value of all assets held by a fund minus liabilities, used to determine the intrinsic value per share or unit.

O

Open-ended funds: Investment funds that continuously issue and redeem shares based on investor demand, requiring constant buying and selling of underlying assets to maintain liquidity.

P

Private capital: The pool of money that is allocated to private markets.

Private credit: Lending provided by non-deposit-taking entities, typically private investment funds, directly financing corporate debt, consumer lending, mezzanine, distressed debt, etc, using investor equity rather than leveraging customer deposits, and offering higher yield and lower liquidity.

Private equity: Investment strategy involving active ownership and management of private companies, typically taking majority stakes acquired via leveraged buyouts (LBOs).

Private markets: Investments made in companies, assets, or projects that are not listed on public exchanges. They include private equity, private credit, venture capital, infrastructure, and real estate.

R

Real asset loans: Private credit investments backed by tangible assets (real estate, infrastructure, commodities), often offering stable and predictable cash flows.

Redemption: Repurchase of securities, shares or units by a company or fund, from an investor.

S

Secondaries market: Transactions involving existing LP interests in closed-end private markets funds, enabling liquidity and portfolio optimisation for investors.

Semi-liquid funds: Evergreen investment vehicles offering contingent redemption rights to investors. Misnomer. See 'Gated evergreens'.

Senior debt: A debt instrument that has a high claim to repayment in the event of default.

Sequential buyout: Term used in this book, otherwise called a 'secondary buyout' – a transaction in which a company is sold from one private equity firm to another.

Subscription lines: Short-term credit facilities secured by LP commitments, providing fund managers flexibility in capital deployment.

Sweat equity: Equity that entrepreneurs and start-up employees take, in place of a salary.

Sweet equity: Equity allocated to managers in an LBO to incentivise and align interests. Often confused with 'sweat equity'.

T

TVPI (Total Value to Paid-in Capital): A measure of how much value a closed-ended fund has created compared with the money investors put in, including both cash returned and the estimated value of what's still in the fund. Presented as a multiple, as in '*That investment return was 3x – thrice the amount invested!*' It does not take into account the time taken to make the return.

V

Valuation leverage (see Multiple arbitrage): Term used in this book to describe the valuation discrepancies between smaller and larger companies, enhancing returns upon sale.

Venture Capital (VC): Early-stage investing in loss-making, sometime pre-revenue, high-growth companies.

Vintage: The year in which a fund is formed or first draws down capital.

Notes

Foreword

1. PitchBook.
2. See LPX Barometer, 2025.

Preface: The Gates are Opening

1. See for example, Larry Fink Chairman's Letter, BlackRock, 2025.
2. For insight into Genghis Khan's strategic and organisational skills, I recommend Genghis Khan and the Making of the Modern World, Jack Weatherford, Broadway Books, Penguin Random House, 2004.

Part I: Foundations

1. If you decide this is the route for you, I would recommend Codie Sanchez's enjoyable and pragmatic *Main Street Millionaire* (2024).

Chapter 1: A Mighty Inheritance

1. John Kay and Mervyn King, *Radical Uncertainty*, (2020) The Bridge Street Press.
2. Encyclopaedia Britannica, in History-Italy, Guiseppe Di Palma https://www.britannica.com/place/Italy/Economy-and-society.
3. For an exploration of this, watch my conversation with Austrian scholar and financier, 'Hans Lovrek on private equity's ancient precedent', 2019, Fund Shack channel, YouTube.
4. Frederic Lane, *Venice: A Maritime Republic*, (1973) John Hopkins University Press.

5. I am led in much of my analysis on the commenda and other ancient partnership agreements, by Richard H Pryor's authoritative essay, 'The Origins of the Commenda Contract'.
6. Stefania Gialdroni, 'Propter Conversationem Diversarum Gentium: Migrating words and merchants in Medieval Pisa', (2020) Legal History Library, Volume 34, Brill | Nijhoff.
7. 'Roma Eterna? Roman rule explains regional well-being divides in Germany', Obschonka et al.; (Current Research in Ecological and Social Psychology, Vol 8, 2025).
8. 'Encyclopaedia Britannica' – Edwin Drake.
9. Robert M Brown, *Journey into Risk Country: The First 30 Years of the Apache Oil Corporation*, (1985) apacorp.com.
10. From 'Bill Draper: The Origins of Venture Capital in Silicon Valley' (Stanford YouTube channel, January 2017).
11. See for example David Graeber's *The Utopia of Rules: On Technology, Stupidity and the Secret Joys of Bureaucracy,* (2015) Melville House Publishing.
12. Daron Acemoglu and James A. Robinson, *Why Nations Fail, The Origins of Power Prosperity and Poverty*, (2012), Crown Publishers, Random House.

Chapter 2: The Enemy Within

1. Berle and Means, *The Modern Corporation and Private Property*, (1932) Harcourt, Brace & Company.
2. For an analysis of the private equity governance model in the context of agency costs, see 'Corporate Governance and Responsible Investment in Private Equity', Simon Witney, Cambridge University Press (2021).
3. Adam Smith, *The Wealth of Nations* (Book V, Chapter 1, 1776) W. Straahan and T. Cadell.
4. Michael Jensen, *Theory of the firm, managerial behaviour, agency costs and ownership structure*, (The Journal of Financial Economics, 1976).
5. 'Deal of the Century: How Michael Dell Turned his Declining PC Business into a $40 Billion Windfall', (Forbes, August 2021).
6. 'Dell Enters into Agreement to Be Acquired by Michael Dell and Silver Lake', (Silver Lake press release, 5 February 2013).
7. 'Analysis of Delaware Supreme Courts Dell Appraisal Decision', Lewkow et al, (December 2017, Harvard Law School Forum).
8. Houlihan Loukey's '2023 Going Private Transaction Study' – based on S&P Capital IQ data) (2022–2023), shows median price premiums of 43–47%.

Chapter 3: Big Beautiful Buyouts

1. For more on this entertaining period, see Carey and Morris, *The King of Capital* (2010).

2. Brown, Gregory W., Christian Lundblad, and William Volckmann. *Inflation Hedging and Real Assets: Are Public and Private Investments the Same?* Working paper, Institute for Private Capital, University of North Carolina, 2024.
3. See, for instance, PEO Partners, run by a Harvard Professor of finance.
4. In the early days (1991–2005) leverage accounted for up to 33% of returns (see, for example, 'Value creation Drivers in Private Equity Buyouts: Empirical Evidence from Europe', Achleitner et al., 2010). But between 2008 and 2018, just 8% of returns were attributed to leverage (see 'Performance Analysis and Attribution with Alternative Investments', Binfare et al., 2022, Institute for Private Capital).

Chapter 6: Risk It for the Biscuit

1. Where r = reproductive rate and k = carrying capacity, or the population that a given environment can sustain.
2. European defense tech start-ups: in it for the long-run? McKinsey, (Feb 2025).

Chapter 7: The Rise of Free Banks

1. McKinsey & Company. (24 Sept. 2024,). 'The Next Era of Private Credit'.
2. Cliffwater.
3. 'Financing the Economy' (The Alternative Investment Management Association, Nov. 2024. Accessed April 2025.)

Chapter 9: Gated Evergreens

1. '2029 Private Market Horizons', PitchBook.
2. Valeria Martinez, 'Early redemption fees are the 'wrong solution' to semi-liquid fund gatings', (Investment Week, March 2024).

Chapter 11: Lost in Liquidity

1. John Kay, *The Kay review of UK equity markets*, (2010).
2. Lietz and Chvanov, *Does the case for private equity still hold?* (Harvard Business School, 2024).
3. Bryan Jenkins, *Portfolio Construction Volume III: Risky Business*, (Hamilton Lane, October 2024).
4. Cyril Demaria-Bengochea, *Shifting the odds: Strategies to invest in private markets*, (Julius Baer, 2025).

Now Pay Homage

If you enjoyed this book, please help us by spreading the word by leaving a review.
Go to https://mybook.to/RossButler
Scroll down to 'Write a review' – even one sentence helps
It's appreciated!
Ross

Index

2 and 20, 130–131
80/20, 6

A

Abbrecht, Todd, 47
Accountability, impact, 33–34
Ackman, Bill, 58
Acquisition finance, 43
Advisory roles, 138
Agency problem, 22
Alignment, 131
Alpha, 128
Altman, Sam, 64
Amadeus, 73
American corporate interests, protection, 24
Analytical tools, 49
Ancillary roles, 138
Anderson, Douglas, 72–73
Anderson, Frederick, 17
Andreesen Horowitz, 74
Angels, 132
Anti-fragile, 86, 103
Apache Oil, 16
AQR Capital Management, 129
Arbitrage, 52–53
  bureaucracy arbitrage, 53
Arpanet, 68
Artificial intelligence (AI)
  adoption, 53
  advancement, support, 85
  disruption, 74
  in-sourcing, 138
  usage, 49, 65
Asian venture capital, buyouts, 128
Asness, Cliff, 129–130
Asset-based finance, fintech company focus, 83–84
Assets
  accumulation, 131
  leasing models, 145–146
  net asset value, discount, 112
  stripping, 145–147
Assets-under-management, growth, 100

Australian Superannuation scheme, 96

B

Balance sheet optimisation, 49
Bank-run, 85
Banks
  bailouts, 79
  banking types, 24–25
  capital requirements, 80
  private partnership, 77
Basel Endgame, 80
Basel III
  implementation, 79–80
  international rules, 79
Behavioural economics, fallacies, 122
Bench demonstrator, 73
Benchmark Capital fund, 62–63
Berkshire Hathaway, 14
Berle, Adolf, 21, 22
Berwin, Stanley J., 18
Big data, deployment, 49
Blackstone (buyout firm), 37
  mega manager, going public, 116–117
  share price, 117
Blackstone Private Credit, 111
Blackstone unlisted real estate income trust (BREIT), 102, 106
Blake, Jonathan, 18–19
Blind pools, 4–5
  LP investment, transparency (absence), 13–14
  purchase issues, 59
Bolt-on acquisitions, 81–82
Bond offerings, standardisation, 78
Bootstrap deals, 25
Bootstrapping techniques, application, 25
Brave New World, A (Huxley), 122
Briggs, Joe, 141, 142
British Home Stores, purchase, 146
Broker-type role, 84
Bureaucracy (bureaucracies)
  arbitrage, 53
  liability management, 78–79

Business
  angels, 62
  investment, 155
Business Development Companies (BDCs), 101, 110–111
  investments, 110
Buy-and-build model, 49–50
Buy the dips, opportunity, 113

C

Call options, 63
Capital
  access, 78
  allocation, 145
  call facilities, short-term loans, 82
  efficiency, improvement, 49
  flow, amount, 79–80
  misallocation, 24
  raising/spending, 57
  return, 57
Capital investment, private markets (usage), 1
Capitalist system, 24
Capital-light businesses, 145
Capital markets, 78
  system, state-sponsored bank underwriting, 79
Carey, David, 38
Carlyle Group, Citibank (joint venture), 83–84
Carried interest, 59, 160
Cashflows, predictability, 39, 85
Cash management tool, 82
C-Corporation structure, 117
Central bank
  liquidity, access, 78
  monetary manipulation, 24
Chew, Donald, 27
Cinven, 53
Closed-ended fund investment, 93
Closed-ended Vehicles, 5, 39
Coca-Cola, 144
Cohen, Leonard, 29
Coinbase, 64
Co-investment, 59–60
Collateralized loan obligations (CLOs)
  banks, relationship, 88
  structuring, 84
Commenda (trust), 10–11
  agreements, usage, 14n1
  contracts, ban, 19
  participation, 15
  translation, 16
Commendator, Limited Partner (comparison), 11
Commitment, cultures, 95–98
Company (companies)
  investment, risk, 61
  loans, 82
  majority share investment, 4
  managers, profit sharing, 5
  undervaluation, 125
  valuation, 43
  value, 4, 83
Conditional liquidity, 99
Confidentiality, 95

Conglomerate, 32
Corporate finance, LBOs, 23
Corporate ownership, stock exchange model, 27
Corporate rehabilitation, 27
Corporate virtue, 67
Covid lockdowns, impact, 57, 103
Creative destruction
  example (Uber), 71
  natural process, 70–71
See Private Credit
Credit funds, evolution, 85–86
Crusades
  First Crusade, 14n1
  Fourth Crusade, 14
Cyber-security, 138

D

Dandolo, Enrico, 14n1
DARPA programme, 69
Day traders, role, 94
Debenhams, buyout, 146
Debt capital markets
  issuance, observation, 78–79
  pandemic lockdown, impact, 79
Debt pressure, avoidance, 40
Debt-structuring skills, 43
Dell Computers
  LBO, 27
  controversy, 28
  leading position, 31
  premium, payment, 30
Dell, Michael, 27–28, 30, 39
Demaria, Cyril, 93–94
Democracy, implications, 155–156
Digital investment platforms, adoption, 97
Digitisation, 49
Dimon, Jamie, 29
Direct credit, 56
Direct-to-company lending, 81–82
Distressed credit, 56
Diversifications, 24, 66
  absence, 134
  alignment, 129
  attraction, 113–115
  need, 74–75
Dividend recap, 41
Doges (Venice), impact, 13
Do-it-yourself (DIY) leverage, application, 42
domestic institutional capital, HNWs (relationship), 96
Draghi, Mario, 85
Drake, Edwin L., 16
Draper, Jr., William Henry, 17
Drexel Burnham, debt sales, 25
Dropbox, 64
Due diligence process, 47
Dynamic economic development, 78

E

Early Stage Venture Capital Limited Partnerships (ESVCLPs), 97

Index

Economic self-interest, constraints (absence), 58
Economy (economies)
　creative destruction, 70–72
　intelligence layer, 64–65
EDHEC Business School, 93
Efficient Markets Hypothesis
　calculus, 48
　fatalism, 53
　incompatibility, 30
Efficient stock markets, company valuation, 43
Emerging managers, talent, 60
End-investors, 136
Enlightened self-interest, 148
Enterprise, stewardship, 8
Environmental, Social, Governance (ESG), 67–68
　platitudes, value, 70
　requirements, 69
　rubric, 148
Environmental Technologies Fund, 64–65
EQT, private equity, 118
Equity bridge finance, 57, 82
Equity bridge financing, 57
Equity gap, creation, 115
Eurazero (listed private equity company), 118
European Investment Fund (EU), 69
European Long-Term Investment Funds (ELTIFs), 102
European mid-market private equity, buyouts, 128
European Union (EU)
　European Investment Fund, 69
　investment companies/trusts, 111
　Sustainability Finance Disclosure Regime, 67
European venture capital, backer, 69
Evergreens, 99
Evidence-based decision making, usage, 6
Exchange-traded funds (ETFs), usage, 29, 102
External advisers, 139–140

F

Fair valuations, 124
Feeder funds, providing, 136
Fees, management, 84–85
Fee-income records, 79
Fiat currency, 40
Fintech companies, focus, 83–84
Flotation, 7–8
Foenus nauticum (sea loans) (Rome), 10
Fonds Communs de Placement dans l'Innovation (FCPI), 97
Fonds d'Investissement de Proximité (FIP), 97
Fragmented markets, rollup, 52
Free banks, appearance, 77
Free market
　detachment, 78
　development, 15
　expectations, 84
Free-market money, 86–87
French private markets fund, creation, 16
Fund commitments
　levels, 56
　portfolio, strategic management, 129
Funding, impact, 145

Funds
　constraints, 57
　diversified pool, 132
　raising, 56
　　qualifications, 141–142
　selector, role, 128
　structure, inefficiency, 51
Funds-of-funds managers, 140

G

Gaither, Rowan, 17
Gated evergreens, 99
　fund selection, 106–107
　offering, 105
　pros/unknowns, 100–101
　provenance, 102–103
　types, 101–102
General Partner (GP)
　financing, 84
　gains, display, 57
　knowledge, limitation, 9
　presence, 5–6
　sale, avoidance, 57
　stakes, 117
　tractator, comparison, 11
Genoa
　invasions, 7
　investment, protection, 14n1
Gere, Richard, 146
Gibson Greeting Cards, buyout, 37
Gigantism, exposure, 80
Global Financial Crisis (GFC), 78–79, 81
　Blackstone, share price, 117
　opportunity, 113
　pre-GFC bull market, Apollo BDC investment, 111
　self-protection effort, 87
Global private capital markets, problems, 127
Glover, Anne, 73
Governance, 129
　alignment, 134
　structures, consistency, 3
　task, 155
Graham, Benjamin, 47
Great convergence, 83–84
Great Depression, 23
　crisis, 78
Green, Philip, 146
Greyball, development, 71
Gross return/net amount, spread, 130
Gross returns, importance, 150–151
Growth
　capital, 137
　potential, investment, 62
Growth-oriented public markets, absence, 69
Guardian, 53

H

Harvard, endowment, 58
Haute finance, 24–25

INDEX

Healthcare
  problem, 144–145
  venture capital, 56
Hedge funds, 58
Hg Capital Trust, 111
Highland charge, 71
High-yield credit market, legitimisation, 88
HNWs, domestic institutional capital (relationship), 96
Holding vehicles, reduction, 29
Houdaille Industries, KKR LBO, 25
Huxley, Aldous, 122

I

Illiquidity
  complexity/confusion, 122
  consideration, 131
  delusion, 122–123
Illiquid listed stocks, 114
Illiquid private assets, ownership, 112
  State guarantee / implicit, 78
Incentives
  alignment, 129
    implications, 131
  fine-tuning, 138
  principles, 131
Individual investors, impact, 153
Inflation-linked assets, 85
Inflation, near-term positive exposure, 40
Information
  age, backbone, 68
  asymmetry, 9
Infrastructure
  funding, 153–154
  funds, 56
Initial public offering (IPO)
  activity, 29
  roadshow, 71
Innovation, social impact, 72
Insider trading, rules, 125–126
In-sourcing, 138
Insurance premium, 150
Intelligence layer, 64–65
Intelligent Investor, The (Graham), 47
Intermediaries, relative performance (obsession), 126
Internal rates of return (IRRs), 83
 value creation teams, 136
Intra-private equity dealmaking, critique, 51
Investing for returns, 67
Investment
  accredited investor temptation, 75
  agreement, ubiquity, 15
  co-investment, 59–60
  companies/trusts, 111
  complexity, 156
  cost, 130
  decision, influences, 94
  hope/optimism, expression, 74
  malinvestment, 79
  management, 90
  productive capital, usage, 79
  radical uncertainty, 10
  riskiness, 10
  time horizon, impact, 94
Bonds
  Investment grade, 56, 85, 87
  risk level, 78
Investors
  angels, 132
  atomised shareholder base, 23
  endemic risk, 132–133
  fund manager partnership, 3
  illiquid assets, performance, 126–128
  role, 55
Islam, venture capital, 12
Isqa contract, 12

J

J-curve, 100
Jensen, Michael, 22
Jobs, quantifiable net impact, 149
Joint-stock companies, Smith observations, 22
Junk bonds, 87
  investors, LBO debt absorption, 25
  lendings, money (providing), 26
Just-in-time finance, 82

K

Kay, John, 8–9
King, Mervyn, 8–9
King of Capital (Carey/Morris), 38
Kohlberg, Jerome, 24–25
Kohlberg, Kravis, Robers (KKR)
  establishment, 47
  formation, 25
  RJR Nabisco acquisition, 38
Kravis, Henry, 25
K-type selectors, suitability, 63

L

Labour, *societas* (partnership), 12
Labour Theory of Value, 130
Large-cap deals, 82
Lending facilities, re-negotiation, 41
Level, 20, 139
Leverage, 23
  Financial engineering, 38
  Financial leverage, 50
  consideration, 131
  effect, 43
  holding, 40–41
  private markets investment feature, 38
  private markets managers usage, 43
  skills, 43
  temptation removal, 40
  valuation leverage, 50
  zero-sum connection, 43
Leveraged buyout (LBO)
  absorption, 25
  acquisition technique, behavioural consequence, 40

buyout boom, 32
carry achievement, 127
emergence, 27
equity, absence, 25
first wave, 87
gross return/net amount, spread, 130
private equity, association, 23
support, 81–82
Lightspeed (Silicon Valley VC), 74
Limited Partner (LP)
  commendator, comparison, 11
  deals, 56
  General Partner, 80/20 basis, 6
  investment, transparency (limitation), 13–14
  presence, 5–6
  returns forecast, 56
  situation, 101
Linear systems, deployment, 9
Liquidity, 121
  escape mechanism, 123
  management, 100–101
  matching, 128
  mismatch risk, 134
Listed managers, impact, 116
Listed private capital, 109
  funds, 110
    share price, function, 112
  managers, 116
Listed private equity company, 118
Loans, syndication, 84
Local communities/businesses, investment, 155
Long-Term Asset Funds (LTAFs), 102
Long-term illiquid asset classes, investment, 102
Long-term interests, alignment, 127
Long-term investment, encouragement, 96
Losses
  minimisation, 46
  risk, 63
Lovefilm (UK), acquisition, 66
Luddite, status, 72
Ludwig, Daniel K., 39
Lump of labour fallacy, 153–154

M

Macro-economic conditions, problems, 127
Magic circle firm, 140
Malinvestment, 79
Management
  consultancies, 136
  fees, impact, 85–86
  teams, behaviour (influence), 40
Managers
  emerging managers, talent, 59–60
  equity ownership, minimum, 22
Mansion House Compact, 104
Market euphoria, impact, 57
Market innovations, 104
Market risk, minimum, 134
Markets, spooking (reason), 126
Marx, Karl, 70
Maturity transformation, 86

McKinsey, 69–70
Means, Gardiner, 21, 22
Meckling, Bill, 22
Mercantilism, 150
Mergers & acquisitions (M&A)
  market, 48
  Meyer, Thomas, ix, xiv
Mezzanine credit, 56
Middle-market lending, 81–82
Mid-market buyouts, 142
Mid-market facilities, 82
Mid-market investors, claim, 46
Mid-market private equity, deals screening, 47
Military spending, impact, 68
Milken, Michael, 25, 87–88
Minority investments, 45
Monetary backing, finiteness, 78
Money lending
  banking type, 24–25
  peer-to-peer/merchant-to-merchant approach, 77
Money loss, risk, 132
Morality, meaning, 148
Moral virtues, equivalence, 78
Morgan, John Pierpont, 77
Morningstar, median return, 105
Morris, John E., 38
Mortgage-backed securities, illiquid loans
  (relationship), 84
Muhammed/Khadijah, marriage, 12
Munger, Charlie, 125
Mutual funds, ease/user-experience, 102

N

Napoleonic Commercial Code (1807), 16
Negotiation, dispute, 95
Net asset value (NAV)
  basis, 101
  credit lines, 82–83
  discounts, 113
  financing, usage, 57
  growth, 105
Netflix, 66
Non-core divisions, sale, 24
Non-linear problems, linear solutions
  (deployment), 9

O

Oil price shock, 24
Oil production, commercialisation, 16
OpenAI, 64
Open-ended evergreens, 97
Operational synergies, benefit, 48
Optos, 73
Origination, 84
Orkin Exterminating Company, management
  control, 39
Outsourcing, 49
Overheads, expense, 148
Oversight, task, 155
Ownership structures, 51–52

P

Pandemic lockdown, impact, 79
Panic premium, 123–125
Parteciaco, Giustiniano (Venice), 10
Partners Group, 102–103
Partnership agreement
  lifespan, finiteness, 14
  power, 6
  private market funds structure, 5–6
  qirad (Islamic partnership agreement), 12
Passive index investing, rationale, 129
Passive property owners, control power (surrender), 22
Paul, Ron, 77
Personality spectrum, 137–138
Personal risk, diversification, 133
Peterson, Jordan B., 143
Piani Individuali di Resparmio (PIR), 97
PitchBook
  market examination, 102
  median return, 105
Playbooks, 52–53
Portfolio
  management, 55
  strategic management, 129
Pricing (optimisation), analytical tools (usage), 49
Primary deals, performance potential, 57
Private bank distribution network, 96
Private companies
  backing, 46
  insider trading, 125
Private credit, 138
  centralised monetary system, relationship, 80
  fund, bank-run (absence), 86
  markets, appearance, 86
Private equity
  CEO preference, 28–30
  commentary/analysis, 150
  competitor, 48
  criticism, 41–42
  deal, 48
  description, 124
  focus, 127
  hands-on, bottom-up nature, 80
  impact, 148–149
  job, 141
  lawyers, earnings, 140
  LBO, logic, 39
  leveraged buyout (LBO), association, 23
  lobby groups, focus, 149
  maturation, 51
  mid-market, impact, 45–46
  ownership
    model, interest (alignment), 32–33
    selection, 32
  people business, 149–150
  reputation, 151
  role, disruptiveness, 147
  strategy, 3
  valuations, impact, 124
  value, 47–48
  vigilance, 151

Private equity backed CFO, 33
Private equity backed companies
  CEO, role/function, 33
  growth, 29
  management teams, behaviour (influence), 40
Private equity firms
  control, 5
  interaction, 52
  operational specialists, involvement, 49
Private equity funds
  financing, 82–83
  investor rewards, 123
  raising, 3–4
  reinvestment, impossibility, 5
Private equity managers
  2 and 20, 130–131
  company undervaluation, 125
  compensation arrangement, 5
  exposure, 133
  financial upside, 126
  freedom/control, 4
  long-term performance, 14
  selection, 32
Private markets
  allocation, 94
  controversy, 154
  description, 48
  diversification attraction, 113–115
  game, avoidance, 144
  individual investors, impact, 153
  initiation, 16–18
  investment, 139
    feature, 38
    strategies, 35
  investors, performance, 127
  language, 128
  outperformance, 129–130
  partnership, 22
  portfolio, 58
  public markets, 21, 26
  real risk, 133–134
  risk, 131–133
  seriousness, 46–47, 90
  success, 9
  usage, 1
  venture capital LP fund, 17
  women, involvement, 139
Private markets funds
  access, 113
  capital, raising/spending, 57
  fees absorption, 42
  forebears, 13
  managers, 136
  mimicry, 42
  opportunities, tactical approach, 57
  partnership agreement structure, 5
  portfolio, management, 55
  solutions, 13
  structures, knowledge (limitation), 18
Private markets managers
  failure, 142
  leverage usage, 43
  lobbying, 104

Index

Private-markets style partnerships, provenance, 19
Private real estate limited partnerships, diversification, 16
Productive capital, usage, 79
Profit-sharing arrangement, power, 19
Property portfolio, value, 146
Public companies
  failures, 43
  operation, characterisation, 21–22
Public disclosure, 148
Public markets
  basis, 30
  building, 41
  contempt, 87
  governance, divergence, 21–22
  growth-oriented public markets, absence, 69
  insider trading, strictness, 126
  intermediaries, 31
  periodic take-privates, 28
  private markets, contrast/comparison, 21, 26
  scrutiny/scepticism, 31
  shareholders, losses, 31
Public pension fund exposure, 96

Q

Qirad (Islamic partnership agreement), 12
Quasi-monopolies, purchase (absence), 41

R

Radical uncertainty, 7–9
RAND Corporation, 17
Real assets loans, 84–85
Real-economy lending, implications, 80
Real estate investment trusts (REITs), 105
Real investment, selection, 155
Recapitalisations, 81–82
Reddit, 64
Redemptions, fulfilment ratio, 105
Remortgage, involvement, 5
Reputation-management, conflation, 148
Resolvable uncertainty, 7–9
Resource-intensive activity, 130
Resources, allocation, 70–71
Returns
  net-returns, 135
  enhancement, 65–66
  Limited Partner (LP) forecast, 56
Risk, 132–133
  determination, 73
  management, 87
  mitigation, 65–66
  perspective, 132
  transfer, immorality, 86
Risk-of-loss concept, 133
Risk-taking, regulator attentiveness, 132–133
RJR Nabisco
  acquisition, 38
  take-downs, 32
Roberts, George, 25
Rockefeller, John D., 16
Rogers, Lois, 95
Roll-out strategy, 50
Rome, fall/invasions, 6
R-type selectors, 63

S

Schumpeter, Joseph, 70
Schwarzman, Stephen, 32, 37, 117
SEB (bank, stakes), 118
Secondaries, 51, 58–59
  funds, allocation, 101
  opportunities, 59
Secondary buyouts, 46 (See Serial Buyouts)
Sector-specialist funds, presence, 56
Selectors
  K-type selectors, suitability, 63
  R-type selectors, 63
Self-fulfilling prophecy, 31–32
Semi-liquid evergreens, 99, 102–103★(See Gated evergreens)
Sequential target, private equity firm takeover, 51–52
Sequoia (Silicon Valley VC), 74
SERIAL BUYOUTS
Shadow banks, 88
Shareholder
  register, reporting, 32
  structure, impact, 8
Share price, function, 112
Sheehan, Patrick, 64–65
Short-term debt, creation, 86
  Loans/Short-term, 82
Siege mentality, 30
Silver Lake, 28
  financial buyer status, problem, 30
  funds, investment, 39
Small Business Act, 68
Small or medium-sized enterprise (SME) consideration, 61–62
Smith, Adam, 22
Socially progressive institutions, wariness, 154
Social mobility, sacrifice, 19
Societas (partnership) (Rome), 12
Sovereign, overextension, 77
S&P Capital IQ, private equity survey, 29
Special situations firm, creation, 17
Auction processes, 48
Stagflation, 24
Standard Oil, formation, 16
Star fund manager
  absence, 128–129
  cult, 129
Start-ups, backing (activity), 67
State-appointed intermediaries, impact, 154
State-owned assets, investment, 46
State-sponsored banks
  commendator, 11
  moral hazard, regulation, 87
  underwriting activity, 79
Stewardship, 8
Stock exchange, companies listing, 22
Stock flotation, 7–8

Stock market
  gatekeepers, 114
  investments, 13–14
  opportunity, shrinkage, 29
  passive index investing, rationale, 129
Stratospheric Aerosol Transport and Nucleation (SATAN), 72n1
Stripe, 64
Sub-asset class
  advertisement, 100–101
  interest, 106
Subject-matter expertise, 49
Sub-lines, Subscription lines, 57, 82
Sustainability Finance Disclosure Regime (EU), 67
Sustainable investment, 67–68
Sweet equity, provision, 33
Swenson, David, 123
Systemic basis, 129

T

Take-privates, 46–47
  value, 28
  wariness, 30
Target Date funds, 104
Taxation
  double layer, 17
  trap, 115
Tender offer vehicles, 101
Thiel, Peter, 63
Third-party managers, opportunities (access), 100
Third-party multi-strategy funds, 100
Thomas H. Lee Partners (THL Partners), 47
Too-big-to-fail mora hazard, 80
Toys 'R' Us, collapse, 147–148
Tractator, General Partner (comparison), 11
Trade
  globalisation, 15
  mechanism, valuation, 10
Trapped cash, unlocking, 49
Trust, breach, 14
Turnaround investments, 146

U

Uber
  aggression, 71–72
  creative destruction example, 71
  go-to-market strategy, assault (effectiveness), 71
Uncertainty, 7–10
Unitranche facilities, 82
Universe, master of, 135, 136
Unlisted evergreens, fund manager, 104
U.S. business development companies (U.S. BDCs), 110–111
U.S. venture capital, outperformance, 69

V

Valuation
  challenges, 87
  leverage, 50

Value
  creators, impact, 80
  drivers, 137
  economic structure extraction, 19
  enhancement, 53
Value, creation
  approach, replication, 52
  plan, usage, 49
  process, 51
Venice
  Doges, impact, 13
  fall, 19
  financing ventures, 11–12
  problems, 7
Venture capital
  deals, 139
  managers, 2 and 20 charges, 130–131
  performance potential, 57
  strategies, variety, 66–67
  term, creation, 17
Venture capital firms
  pickiness, 62
  risk mitigation/returns enhancement, 65–66
Venture capital funds, 75
  marketing, 72–73
  returns, 66–67
Venture capitalists (VCs)
  characteristics, 68
  focus, 67
  returns, making, 63
Venture Capital Trusts (VCT), tax incentives, 115
Venture debt, 82
Venture statism, 68–70
Vested interests, allegiance, 70–71
Vintages, 127
  exposure, 56
Viridiuim, 53
Volatility
  buy the dips opportunity, 113
  creation, public markets (impact), 124
  private equity valuations, impct, 124

W

Waterman Steamship Corporation, Ludwig acquisition, 39
Wealth
  creation, 27
  soaking, 136
Wesray, buyout shop, 37
Woodford, Neil, 114–115
World War II, crisis, 78

Y

Y Combinator, 64

Z

Zero-sum, 15, 42, 66
Zero to One (Thiel), 63
Zombie companies, problems, 32

A SUMMARY OF RERUM NOVARUM OR ON CAPITAL AND LABOR

AN INTRODUCTION TO AND
PARAGRAPH-BY-PARAGRAPH SUMMARY
OF *RERUM NOVARUM* BY POPE LEO XIII

BY OMAR F. A. GUTIÉRREZ

NO. 1 IN THE CATHOLIC SOCIAL TEACHING SERIES

For Miriam

Nihil Obstat
Rev. Matthew J. Gutowski, S.T.L.
Censor librorum

Imprimatur
Most Reverend George J. Lucas
Archbishop of Omaha
June 10, 2020
Omaha, NE

© 2020 Omar F. A. Gutiérrez

No part of this book may be reproduced, stored on a retrieval system, or transmitted in any form or by any means, electronic, mechanical, photocopying, or otherwise, without the prior written permission of the author, except by a reviewer, who may quote brief passages in a review.

Excerpts from *Rerum Novarum*
are from the English translation.
Copyright © Libreria Editrice Vaticana.
Used by permission. All rights reserved.

ISBN-13: 979-8-6686197-4-0

Printed in the United States of America

Introduction

Catholic Social Teaching is a set of doctrines based on certain fundamental values. It provides principles for reflection, criteria for judgment, and guidelines for action. These principles, criteria, and guidelines have developed since the late nineteenth century in response to concrete historical circumstances, which have served as the backdrop for the teaching's pastoral, practical approach.

In this first of a series of introductions to the social documents, we look at *Rerum Novarum* (1891) and to the one hundred years before Pope Leo XIII wrote this foundation encyclical for Catholic Social Teaching. In that century, a series of groundbreaking revolutions occurred simultaneously, and they forced the Catholic Church to provide a robust response.

The Philosophical Revolution

The Enlightenment marks the emergence of man's confidence in his ability to know and dominate the universe through his rational capacities. The characters of this period, such as Voltaire, Diderot, Rousseau, and many more, argue that faith and organized religion are obstacles to the pursuit of truth. Immanuel Kant (d. 1804) argues that a comprehensive moral system, knowable by the human intellect and based on rational thought without the assistance of Divine Revelation, is possible and should be pursued.

Fredrich Hegel (d. 1831) maintains this position while advancing the dialectic method, and Auguste Comte (d. 1857) creates the social sciences replacing God and Catholicism with humanity and humanism. Ludwig Feuerbach (d. 1872) adopts an avowedly atheist philosophy inspiring Karl Marx's (d. 1883) rejection of God in favor of a materialist interpretation of society under the rubric of class struggle. Finally, Friedrich Nietzsche (d. 1900) fingers Christianity as the source of our social ills, produces *Beyond Good and Evil* in 1886, and calls for an *Übermensch*, a "superman," who lives above the morals of the average man by creating his own moral universe.

In one hundred years or so, the philosophical trends that shaped the world's leaders shifted from a marriage between faith and reason, to a confidence in rational, universal moral systems suspect of organized religion, to the total rejection of God in favor of "the will to power."

The Political Revolution

During this same one-hundred-year transformation of philosophical thinking, the American Revolution starts us off in 1776 unseating Great Britain as the unassailable powerhouse of the world. The French Revolution starts in 1789. The Italian effort toward unification begun in 1815 is a revolution against various powers but particularly the Vatican. Otto von Bismarck (d. 1898), while not the head of a revolution against an existing State government, worked to unify all the German-speaking people: Germans, Bavarians, Czechs, and Prussians, among others. Revolutions in the New World against Spain and Portugal erupted as well. The way people related to their governments and saw their role in those governments changed drastically. This is also the time of the rise of nationalism. Napoleon (d. 1821) emerges, and the first modern wars of European nation-states take place.

Much of this, and the revolution of philosophy, was made possible by another revolution that was happening at exactly the same period of time before *Rerum Novarum*. The leisure necessary for widespread reading and philosophical thought; the uniforms, guns, and complicated mechanisms for war; the feeling that everything was in flux but that humankind was at the forefront of a new frontier of ever-beneficial progress; the idea that we were controlling the reigns of history – it was all possible thanks to the Industrial Revolution.

The Industrial Revolution

In what must have seemed like the blink of an eye, the way the average European provided for his family, participated in the local economy, and understood the organization of social wealth changed radically. While it is true that there was a great deal of wealth creation during the Industrial Revolution, it cannot be denied that a great deal of damage was done during this time to intermediary institutions like the guilds and the family.

Masses of poorly educated workers became concentrated in the cities. Hordes of laborers were forced to work in dangerous, unregulated factories and to live in inhuman and squalid conditions. Men, women, and children labored without contracts and could be fired at any moment. They worked long hours earning pitiful wages. A laborer's connection to his work, that is, his sense that his work was an extension of his self, evaporated in the repetitive actions of the factory. Factory work was in a sense mindless work and so ceased to be human work. Labor had been disconnected from human dignity, and the laborer became a commodity. This is the world of Charles Dickens (d. 1870) and of Victor Hugo (d. 1885). This is the world where the poor and the vulnerable fell through every crack.

Successful industrialists had access to massive amounts of wealth and the political and social connections that came with it. This wealth creation provided for a perhaps more democratic distribution of influence and power. However, while aristocratic structures in society were flawed, nobles were taught by tradition and by faith that they had a deep responsibility to help the poor who were falling through those cracks. This was not necessarily so for the industrialists. Their wealth was earned, not inherited; thus, no responsibility toward others seemed obviously apparent.

The Church

The Catholic Church in this same period suffered attacks and marginalization. During the September Massacres of September 2 and 3, 1792, more than two hundred priests, bishops, and abbots were slaughtered along with about one thousand other political prisoners by French revolutionists. It took two days because the murderous mob needed to rest and procure more alcohol to feed their rage. They committed the crimes because they viewed the Church as the enemy of their necessary progress toward liberty and fraternity.

The martyrs of Compiègne, immortalized in the opera *Dialogue of the Carmelites* by Francis Poulenc, were sixteen Carmelite nuns guillotined for being Catholic. St. Jeanne Jugan (d. 1879), as a young, French girl, wrote in her diaries about how visiting priests celebrated Mass and baptized children at night in the barns for fear of the revolutionist authorities.

Then there was the persecution of Catholics in Germany. Otto von Bismarck's desire to unify all German-speaking peoples was resisted by the Catholic population. They were not interested in centralized government much less one run by Protestants. But von Bismarck would not be thwarted. He mounted a *kulturkampf*, a "culture war," against Catholics and anyone else who resisted. He shut down monasteries, convents, and seminaries. He refused travel rights and other basic human rights to Catholics. As a result, many were forced to flee.[1]

The hierarchy suffered as well. Pope Pius VI (d. 1799) was kidnapped by one of Napoleon's generals and was pressed to renounce his temporal authority. Eventually, the frail pontiff died as he put off the diminutive general. Pius VII (d. 1823) spent much of his pontificate trying, mostly unsuccessfully, to keep Napoleon from invading other Catholic countries. Pope Leo XII (d. 1829) was well meaning but was considered by all to have been hapless in his attempts to understand what was going on in Europe. He was succeeded by Pope Pius VIII (d. 1830), who lasted just under two years before his spirit and body were crushed by the pressures of the time. Pope Gregory XVI (d. 1846) did his best but managed to ruffle the feathers on all sides for and against the Church.

Pope Pius IX (d. 1878) was at first called a "liberal pope." He had released political prisoners the Church had arrested during the revolutionary efforts in the Papal States. When those released prisoners promptly tried to kill him, the liberal pope changed and eventually came to be known as one of the most rigid in the Church's modern history. He is most famous for the "Syllabus of Errors," a handy list of the errors of the age which he provided to the world's bishops. It ends with the following statement: "The Roman Pontiff can, and ought to, reconcile himself, and come to terms with progress, liberalism and modern civilization."[2] This is an error. Therefore, the opposite position is to be taken by the Catholic: the pope does not have to accept modern civilization. Period. His approach has been described as trying to shut the Church off from the world. While the Church's chief shepherd wanted to withdraw, many wanted to engage.

Social Catholicism

The rest of the Church initially began to address the new circumstances through a combination of charitable works and an invitation to new modes of cooperation. Direct assistance was provided through hospitals and schools. St. Jean-Baptiste de La Salle (d. 1719) in France remade education in order to serve the poor children left behind by the industrialization that decimated families. St. John Bosco (d. 1888) and the Salesians worked in Turin, the industrial epicenter of Italy, again with young people who found themselves essentially parentless. But lay men and women were also greatly involved. Blessed Frédéric Ozanam (d. 1853) founded the Society of St. Vincent de Paul to help organize charitable efforts for the poor in Paris and beyond. Venerable Pauline Jaricot (d. 1862) founded the Pontifical Society for the Propagation of the Faith to help spread the Gospel to all parts of the world, including the still young Americas.

But charitable work was not the only method of answering these problems. There was the stellar example of Léon Harmel (d. 1915). The head of a textile factory, he viewed his role as owner to be also the father and protector of his workers. He created for them a labor union and provided them a health clinic, an elementary school for their children, and training on wealth management. He organized a pilgrimage to Rome to celebrate the laborer and encouraged the cooperation of local intermediary institutions to work with each other for the benefit of the common good.

Meanwhile, some bishops were formulating conceptual and practical answers to the "social question." That phrase, used by many at the time, referred to the dramatic increase of poverty, the breakdown of social structures like the family and the guilds, and the concentration of wealth in the hands of a very few. Gaspard Cardinal Mermillod (d. 1892) battled persecution in Switzerland in order to form the Union of Fribourg, in which he gathered the ablest thinkers and activists of his area so as to address the "social question." In France, Bishop Jean Paul Alban de Villeneuve-Bargemont (d. 1850) wrote against ethically challenged industrialists by encouraging the just wage and other obligations of employers toward their employees. In Germany, Bishop Wilhelm von Ketteler (d. 1877) articulated many of the problems with Socialist attempts to solve the "social question." He also encouraged Catholics to start to live a "social Catholicism" that would create numerous intermediary institutions from which they could find support and which could serve as a buffer against the ills of the age.

Pope Leo XIII

On February 20, 1878, Cardinal Gioacchino Pecci was elected Pope Leo XIII (d. 1903), succeeding Pope Pius IX. He was in his late sixties at the time, and his health was poor. Leo was sometimes referred to by friends as a soul dragging around a body as he rarely slept and ate very little. The consensus was that he would have a brief reign after the thirty-two-year pontificate of the previous pope. But that soul and that body helped to support a brilliant mind that would reign for twenty-five years. And for this new modern world, he was eager to provide a Catholic vision that was not tucked behind bastions but rang out with the power of truth.

The Holy Father would write a total of eighty encyclicals. In the lead up to *Rerum Novarum*, he covered such topics as the foundational importance of the family, the nature of human liberty, the role of the State, the responsibilities of the Christian citizen, and the follies of Socialism. Through all of them, it was clear that the Holy Father was keenly interested in the "social question." So it was that, though he was eighty-one years old, Pope Leo began to write *Rerum Novarum*, the encyclical that would usher a new era into the Church.

One of the first things he did was to consult those who had been working on the "social question" for years. He consulted Villeneuve-Bargemont, Mermillod, and von Ketteler, whom he revered. He even consulted Harmel the business owner. He understood that the answer to the difficulties of his age could not be simply theoretical. This was a pastoral effort to be implemented, not just a matter of doctrinal formulations to be studied in private.

In the end, he saw the difficulties of his age as a series of revolutions, hence the first words of the encyclical. The Latin language has no one word for "revolution" in the sociopolitical sense. The closest thing is *res novae* or "new things." But because it was precisely the various revolutions of the time about which Pope Leo was writing, *rerum novarum* is translated as "revolutionary" in the opening words of the document, for indeed, the times were revolutionary.

Pope Leo XIII's *Rerum Novarum* was received with great praise. Having condemned Socialism and endorsed labor unions, Catholics in every nation were emboldened to form their collectives and to fight for worker rights. The Catholic Church, long hated in Europe and in the United States, would become a moral leader in the worldwide effort to bring more justice into the new governments and economies of the time. With *Rerum* the pope demonstrates that the Church is not only interested in the next life but also in the lives of the poor and suffering of today. What's more, the Church's interest in the poor and in government translates into real initiatives and plans to help rebuild society along the values of the Gospel. This document from 1891 would be the hinge upon which many, though not all, later developments of the social teaching would be built. It is considered the beginning year of modern Catholic Social Teaching.

Paragraph-by-Paragraph Summery

The student of the social teaching should always be encouraged to read the full text of the constitutive documents. Admittedly, some are easier to read than others. Pope Leo XIII's style is eminently readable. Still, the long, Ciceronian sentences typical of the time can be frustrating to some readers. The following paragraph-by-paragraph summary is meant only as a quick guide to aid reading the text itself. It is not meant as a total replacement for reading as it is not exhaustive of the wonderful teaching given by Pope Leo XIII in this foundational encyclical. Still, quotations from the official English translation of the text have been provided in order to convey more precisely the language and feeling of Pope Leo.

Introduction

1. The spirit of revolution in the field of capital and labor is on everyone's mind.

2. As we have discussed other topics, "truth and justice" demand that we address these topics of rights and duties so that further revolution can be avoided.

3. What is absolutely clear is that
   a. something must be done for the workers who are suffering;
   b. guilds, which have disappeared, cannot protect the worker;
   c. States and "public institutions" have rejected the faith;
   d. wealth is in the hands of the few, which creates a new kind of slavery.

I. Socialism's Answer

4. Socialists offer an answer by removing private property. This is wrong and would cause the workers to suffer first.

5. Property, or capital, is simply wages in another form. Thus, Socialism strikes at the heart of what labor is for, that is, the free use of what one has earned.

6. This Socialist principle against private property is against the virtue of justice. Private property is a

natural right. Indeed, permanent possession of things is part of what humans require for life.

7. Furthermore, man's needs extend into the future, which means he requires planning, which means he requires long-term *possession* of capital. Nature provides man's needs through the earth and its fruits. Man, therefore, does not need the State. Man "precedes the State, and possesses, prior to the formation of any State, the right of providing for the substance of his body."

8. God allows for private property. Still, we are not allowed to use it however we want. There are limits that are "fixed by man's own industry, and by the law of the individual races."

9. Another proof of the right to private property is that man "leaves, as it were, the impress of his personality" on that on which he labors. Thus, he must be allowed ownership of the thing.

10. This is all so obvious it is odd that the Socialist answer cannot see this truth. The fruit of one's labor belongs to the laborer.

11. The respect for private property is, in fact, "the most unmistakable manner to the peace and tranquility of human existence." Divine law even confirms this in the ninth and tenth commandments.

12. The need to provide for a family further makes this right to private property necessary. Since man is

called to raise families and families are "older than any State," man has a right to provide for his society the family.

13. The right to private property becomes firmer with the increased size of the family. And looking to the future, if the father cannot own property, how can he pass on capital to his family? "The family must necessarily have rights and duties which are prior to those of the community."

14. The State, therefore, cannot have control over the family. The contrary is a "great and pernicious error." Certainly, public aid for needy families ought to be in place. The State may step in to end certain abuses. "But the rulers of the commonwealth must go no further." The Socialist answer results in the destruction of the "structure of the home."

15. This main tenet of Socialism, the "community of goods," can only result in envy, a disincentivizing of labor, and nothing else but equal misery.

16. In truth, "no practical solution of this question will be found apart from the intervention of religion and of the Church." The Church is the keeper of the Gospel, which provides the key to solving the conflict between men. The Gospel not only "enlightens the mind" but also gives practical directives for daily life. Furthermore, the Church does already improve the working conditions of laborers around the world "by means of numerous organizations."

II. The Role of the Church

17. The first thing to note is the reality of the situation. Absolute, material equality is not possible or even beneficial to society.

18. All human existence on this earth involves suffering and sacrifice. Those who sell to those who suffer "the boon of freedom from pain and trouble, an undisturbed repose, and constant enjoyment – they delude the people and impose upon them, and their lying promises will only one day bring forth evils worse than the present." Seek outside of this earthly existence for real answers.

19. One of the greatest mistakes to avoid is presuming class warfare is necessary. Each needs the other: "capital cannot do without labor, nor labor without capital." The Church is particularly good at bringing "the rich and the working class together" by reminding each of its respective duties.

20. These are the duties of the "proletarian and the worker":
    a. to do the work agreed upon well;
    b. never to injure the property or person of the employer;
    c. never to engage in violence or disorder to defend one's cause;
    d. not to associate with hucksters.

The following are the duties of the "wealthy owner and the employer":

a. to view every worker with dignity and not as a "bondsmen";

b. to know that working for gain is "creditable";

c. to know that to misuse men, to view them as means to an end, is "truly shameful and inhuman";

d. in dealing with workers, their religion and souls ought to be kept in mind
   i. to make sure they have time to fulfill religious duties,
   ii. to protect them from corruption and "dangerous occasions,"
   iii. to not lead them away from their families,
   iv. to encourage them away from squandering their earnings;

e. do not overly tax employees;

f. do not give employees labor that is "unsuited to their sex and age";

g. give them a just wage
   i. to gather profit from the need of others (i.e., the indigent or destitute) is against human/divine law,
   ii. to defraud someone of a just wage is a crime that calls for vengeance from Heaven,
   iii. the employer may not cut the wages by force, fraud, or usury.

21. The Church "aims higher still," however. The Christian is driven by thoughts of everlasting life in determining how best to live. Without "the idea of futurity," there is no right or wrong. Riches are not the end but rather "to use them aright."

22. Those who do have riches ought to be warned about their danger, for riches are an obstacle to "eternal happiness" and thus to freedom. These are some fundamental truths about ownership:

    a. As the ancients taught, the right to own is different from "a right to use money as one wills."

    b. The Church teaches that our possessions are not ours but really God's and so must be used "without hesitation when others are in need."

    c. We are not required to distribute what we need to live or to maintain what is "becoming," but from what remains we ought to give. This is charity.

    d. "To sum up, then, what has been said: Whoever has received from the divine bounty a large share of temporal blessings, whether they be external and material, or gifts of the mind, has received them for the purpose of using them for the perfecting of his own nature, and, at the same time, that he may employ them, as the steward of God's providence, for the benefit of others."

23. We also know from Christ that poverty is no disgrace.

24. This shows us that the true value of a man is not wealth but rather "virtue, and virtue alone, wherever found."

25. With this Christian perspective, then, a true equality can be sought because class warfare is removed.

26. The Church, furthermore, provides the opportunities and the training in virtue necessary for bringing about this true equality within society.

27. Indeed a look at history demonstrates the help that the Church has offered over time, bringing "from death to life" previously dying societies. By bringing societies back to their basic principles, the Church can heal. The current situation really cannot be healed without the aid of the Church.

28. This is not to say, however, that the Church is only concerned with the spiritual needs of the people. She does care for the poor. But She also recognizes that, when a society is morally upright, this "leads itself to temporal prosperity, for it merits the blessing of that God who is the source of all blessing."

29. In fact, the Church has and does and will continue to do charitable work. She has a reputation for it.

30. Some argue that the State ought to take over the work that the Church does, but no one can make up for the "self sacrifice of Christian charity."

31. At the same time, this does not mean that the State has no role. "It is sufficient, therefore, to inquire what part the State should play in the work of remedy and relief."

III. The Role of the State

32. As I wrote in *On the Christian Constitution of the State*, the State's laws must be enacted for the common good and for "private prosperity." By giving particular care for the needs of the working class, there will be less need to give them special help. The general welfare is met through:
   a. moral rule,
   b. well-regulated family life,
   c. respect for religion and justice,
   d. moderate and fair public taxes,
   e. the progress of arts and trades,
   f. fruitful harvests,
   g. essentially, anything "which makes the citizens better and happier."

33. Since the working class is largely in the majority, and since the State has the obligation to maintain the common good, it only makes sense that the State focus on the needs of the working class first so as to be able to meet the needs of all the other classes. This is called "distributive" justice.

34. There will always be differences between classes. All contribute to the common good, just not in the same way. For those who are more directly in charge of the common good, that is, politicians, they need to keep in mind the following: since "the end of society is to make men better," then public life ought to be structured so as to make it easier for "virtuous action." The chief condition for such a public life is the working conditions of the working

class. Justice for the worker is in the best interest of the State, for "it is only by the labor of working men that States grow rich."

35. Though the State cannot absorb the family into itself, there is still a role for the State to care for the safety of the community.

36. This in mind, when there are violations of the common good by families, employers, or workers, the State has a role in correcting the wrong. "The principle being that the law must not undertake more, nor proceed further, than is required for the remedy of the evil or the removal of the mischief."

37. In this effort, then, the State ought to give special care to the poor and the working class, who "have no resources of their own to fall back upon," when they find themselves victims.

38. The State must also protect the private property of the workers from those who would take advantage of them through thievery, from greedy employers, and from revolutionaries who "stir up disorder and incite their fellows to acts of violence."

39. Strikes are usually the result of too much labor, excessively hard labor, or insufficient wages. If the State addresses these things, then it can keep the peace.

40. The State, too, should protect men's souls. Life on earth is not "the final purpose for which man is

created." To be an obstacle in man's pursuit of eternal life is to violate God's rights, not just man's, for their souls are God's.

41. Therefore, the State ought to help workers to keep holy the Sabbath, which does not mean idleness or spending money "for vicious indulgence."

42. The State ought also to try to secure proper working conditions for the workers. This involves the number of hours worked, where one works, the nature of the work, and the health and strength of the workman. The time, place, and nature of the work ought to account for the sex and age of the workers as well. Furthermore, the employer and the worker cannot agree to give up on the duties the worker owes to God and to himself. Man is not free to harm himself.

43. Now we come to the question of a just wage. What is generally said is that if the worker and the employer both agree to a wage, then it must be a just wage. Violations are relegated, then, to when the employer does not pay or the worker does not work.

44. This is not a complete analysis, however. Labor has two realities to it. It is personal, that is, bound up with his personality. It is also *necessary*, that is, required for the maintenance of life. If it were just personal, then the current view of just wage would be fine. However, since it is *necessary*, the current view fails, for the worker has the right to pursue that

which guarantees his life. These two aspects are inseparable. "It necessarily follows that each one has a natural right to procure what is required in order to live, and the poor can procure that in no other way than by what they can earn through their work."

45. A just wage ought to be able to support a frugal worker, but injustices do occur. When they do, "in order to supersede undue interference on the part of the State," recourse ought to be sought from associations about which we will soon talk.

46. For now, if the wage is sufficient, the worker can support himself and the family. With frugality he can save and with time perhaps become an owner, which is highly encouraged.

47. With more ownership of land or capital, greater equality can be attained among the various classes. This helps to close the wide gap between the wealthy and the poor. Another advantage to ownership is that men tend to work harder for that which they own. This would also help get rid of the problem of emigration, for the worker would wish to stay in his own nation if he were invested in the capital of his homeland. Of course, this all requires that the State enact a just taxation system that does not "deprive the private owner of more than is fair."

48. Employers and workers can do much to affect the condition of workers by participating in associations that can bring the two classes together.

49. Unions are key to such an effort. They are, like the guilds in the past, of great use for workers as well as their craft. Some of these unions already exist. Let us address them and their rights and duties.

IV. Role of the Unions/Associations

50. Mankind knows that our own weaknesses require the community of others for help. This is how civil societies are formed and thus associations like these as well.

51. These associations are distinct from the State in that they have different ends. The State is concerned with the general welfare, the common good. The association, however, is concerned with the private good of the members of the association. Since their end meets the natural need of men to associate with each other for aid and such right to association precedes the State, they cannot be prohibited by the State.

52. Now, of course, if the association exists to harm the common good and/or attack the State, the State can take measures to protect itself and society.

53. There has been a long history in the Church of "confraternities, societies, and religious orders" over the centuries, and they have done good things. The State ought not have any control over them. When constitutions claim that association is free to all and yet Catholic associations are attacked and hampered,

we must point out that States have not met their obligation, and we decry the double standard that has been used against the Church.

54. There are actually some associations, some secret societies, that exist to harm men's souls and speak out against the Church. Obviously, Christian working men ought to avoid such associations and perhaps start their own.

55. Great praise ought to be given to many of those Catholics who have worked to better the condition of workers. Bishops ought to support such work. The State should foster such associations but not involve itself too deeply for fear of spoiling it.

56. Associations should be wisely administered.

57. They ought to be allowed to exist in societies in order to help develop the humanity of the worker in the areas of body, soul, and property. The chief of these is the soul because it does not profit a man to have property but lose his soul.

58. The association ought to be structured according to the betterment of its members. It should have good and prudent leaders and a fair administration of common funds, and it should keep the rights and duties of the workers *and* the employers in mind. When there are labor disputes, it should set up committees to help come to an equitable agreement. At all times work should be found for its members,

and a fund should be set up for the needs of the workers and their families.

59. In ancient times Christians were looked down upon for being poor, but their charity eventually won society over.

60. If Christians create these associations, then despite the obvious prejudice today, they will win over their fellow citizens.

61. With so many of the working class who have lost hope in the despair of injustice, Christian associations can provide not just the practical answers to the problems but also balm to the heart "by helping them out of their difficulties, inviting them to companionship and receiving the returning wanderers to a haven where they can securely find repose."

V. Conclusion

62. All of this being said, again, the main thing is the need for religion, for only the Gospel can destroy evil at its root.

63. The Church will always be found available to help society. For this reason, the bishops need to promote true charity, that law of the Gospel, the "surest antidote against worldly pride and immoderate love of self."

64. Blessings.

[1] This is in part why many Catholic parishes and religious communities of German descent in the U.S. were founded in the late 1800s. Having fled Europe, they came to America for broader religious liberties.

[2] Pope Pius IX did not write the "Syllabus of Errors" or sign it. It is a list of summary statements compiled by his secretary, Cardinal Antonelli. The statements are based upon papal bulls written by Pope Pius IX, which are referenced at the end of each statement. This is why St. John Henry Cardinal Newman states in his "Letter to the Duke of Norfolk" that the Syllabus is authoritative only to the extent that it reflects the full teaching of the original documents. The list itself has "no dogmatic force." See William E. Gladstone and John Henry Newman, *Newman and Gladstone: The Vatican Decrees* (Notre Dame: University of Notre Dame Press, 1962), 153.

Printed in Great Britain
by Amazon